British Railways
The First 25 Years

Volume 12
London Eastern Region

There are several boys leaning out of the windows as L&NER built 'N7/3' 0-6-2T No. 69702 passes Manor Road sidings and coal yard immediately after leaving Stoke Newington station with the 1.30pm Liverpool Street-Enfield on Saturday 4th April 1959. The train is the typical formation of two 'Quint-Arts', the five-coach articulated sets built for the Great Eastern "Jazz" suburban services in the mid-1920s.

K.L. Cook / Rail Archive Stephenson

BRITISH RAILWAYS

The First 25 Years
Volume 12 – London Eastern Region

J. Allan and A. Murray

Lightmoor Press

Class '55' No. 9011 *The Royal Northumberland Fusiliers* is ready to depart with the 09.35 King's Cross-Edinburgh on 20th May 1973. It is a Sunday morning and at least one platform track is out of use.

Cover photographs

Front upper: Gresley 'A3' 4-6-2 No. 60052 *Prince Palatine* departs from Marylebone with the 'Master Cutler' to Sheffield Victoria in 1949.
F.R. Hebron/Rail Archive Stephenson

Front lower: An 'N2' 0-6-2T waits as Peppercorn 'A1' 4-6-2 No. 60118 *Archibald Sturrock* makes a vigorous start from King's Cross on 31st December 1953. Pacifics and 'N2' 0-6-2Ts were characteristic of the station for three decades. At the front of the express is one of the former 'West Riding' streamliner Brake Third twins.

Back upper: 'A2/2' 4-6-2 No. 60502 *Earl Marischal* at King's Cross 'Top Shed' alongside *Flying Scotsman* on 31st October 1954. It had been rebuilt from a Gresley 'P2' 2-8-2 in 1944, replacing the Gresley conjugated valve gear with three independent sets of motion.

Back centre: The passengers waiting for their train watch Brush Type '2' No. D5593 as it passes through Stratford with an Up express soon after entering service in February 1960. The first three coaches are from three different eras, Gresley, Thompson and British Railways, which was typical at this time.

Back lower: GER 'F5' 2-4-2T No. 67193 with the Ongar push-and-pull at Epping on 1st April 1956. No. 67193 was withdrawn along with the other engines which were used on the service after the electrification of the line from Epping to Ongar was completed in November 1957.

© Lightmoor Press, J. Allan, A. Murray, 2023.
Designed by Ian Pope.

British Library Cataloguing-in-Publication Data.
A catalogue record for this book is available from the British Library.
ISBN 978-1-915069-19-1

All rights reserved. No part of this publication may be reproduced, stored in a retrieval system or transmitted in any form or by any means, electronic, mechanical, photocopying, recording or otherwise, without the written permission of the publisher.

LIGHTMOOR PRESS
Unit 144B, Lydney Trading Estate, Harbour Road,
Lydney, Gloucestershire GL15 4EJ
www.lightmoor.co.uk

Lightmoor Press is an imprint of
Black Dwarf Lightmoor Publications Ltd.

Printed in Poland
www.lfbookservices.co.uk

Contents

Introduction and Acknowledgements	7

1 King's Cross — 8
- The station — 9
- From nationalisation until 1957 — 11
- Suburban services — 17
- Freight — 19
- 1960s – steam bows out as diesels take over — 20
- Diesel prototypes — 24
- Diesels 1958-1966 — 27
- British Rail 1968-1975 — 32
- The Engine Yard aka 'Passenger Loco' — 35

2 Metropolitan Widened Lines — 37
- King's Cross/York Road — 37
- Farringdon — 40
- Aldersgate — 41
- Moorgate — 42

3 King's Cross to New Barnet — 45
- Belle Isle — 45
- Copenhagen Tunnel — 49
- Holloway — 51
- Finsbury Park — 56
- Harringay (West) — 59
- Hornsey and Ferme Park — 65
- Wood Green — 70
- New Southgate — 75
- Oakleigh Park — 76
- New Barnet — 78

4 Great Northern line engine sheds — 79
- King's Cross 'Top Shed' — 79
- Hornsey — 82
- Finsbury Park — 85

5 Finsbury Park-Alexandra Palace/East Finchley — 87
- Crouch End — 87
- East Finchley — 87
- Cranley Gardens — 88
- Muswell Hill — 89
- Alexandra Palace — 89

6 Marylebone — 90
- At nationalisation — 91
- 1950s — 94
- Early 1960s — 96
- The London Midland Region take over — 98
- Servicing point — 99

7 Neasden — 100
- Station — 100
- Main line shed — 102
- London Transport Neasden depot — 105

8 The North London line — 106
- Graham Road — 106
- Dalston Junction — 107
- Canonbury — 108
- Highbury & Islington — 110

9 Liverpool Street — 111
- The station — 112
- From nationalisation until 1955 — 113
- The "Jazz" service — 119
- Late 1950s and 1960s — 121
- Electrification — 124
- Diesels — 125

10 Liverpool Street approaches — 128
- Bethnal Green — 128
- Hackney Downs — 133
- Stratford station — 136

11 Stratford Shed, Works and Temple Mills yard — 146
- The Shed — 146
- Steam days — 147
- Diesel shunters — 151
- Dieselisation — 154
- Works — 156
- Temple Mills — 160
- Lea Bridge — 162

12 Stratford to Ilford — 163
- Maryland — 164
- Manor Park — 164
- Ilford — 165

13 Hackney Downs to Brimsdown — 168
- Clapton — 168
- Copper Mill Junction — 170
- Tottenham South Junction — 171
- Northumberland Park — 172
- Angel Road — 172
- Ponders End — 174
- Brimsdown — 174

14 Hackney Downs to Chingford — 175
- Clapton — 175
- Hoe Street — 176
- Wood Street — 176
- Chingford — 178

15 Hackney Downs to Enfield Town — 180
- Rectory Road — 180
- Stoke Newington - Manor Road — 181
- Seven Sisters — 183
- Lower Edmonton — 185
- Enfield Town — 185

16 Stratford to Palace Gates — 188
- Seven Sisters — 188
- Noel Park and Wood Green — 189
- Palace Gates (Wood Green) — 190

17 Stratford to North Woolwich — 191
- Stratford Low Level — 191
- Stratford Market — 193
- Canning Town — 195
- Abbey Mills Junction — 196
- Thames Wharf Junction — 197
- North Woolwich — 198

18 Stratford to Epping and Ongar — 201
- Leytonstone — 201
- Loughton — 202
- Epping — 202
- North Weald — 205
- Blake Hall — 206
- Ongar — 207

In front of the classic Liverpool Street skyline, the design that revolutionised Great Eastern express services, 'Britannia' 4-6-2 No. 70007 *Coeur-de-Lion* waits to depart with an express for Norwich in 1951. Note the hollow axles on the coupled wheels which saved 2cwt. per wheelset and the fluted coupling rods. These were replaced with solid axles and stronger plain section coupling rods after a series of incidents in mid-1951 which were traced to the coupled wheels shifting on their axles. The most high profile involved 70004 at Headcorn while working the 'Golden Arrow' on 27th October which resulted in a broken connecting rod. All twenty-five engines in service were immediately withdrawn and investigations showed that this was a problem on designs with roller bearings. Note the first coach, a Thompson TK, is still in L&NER painted teak livery.

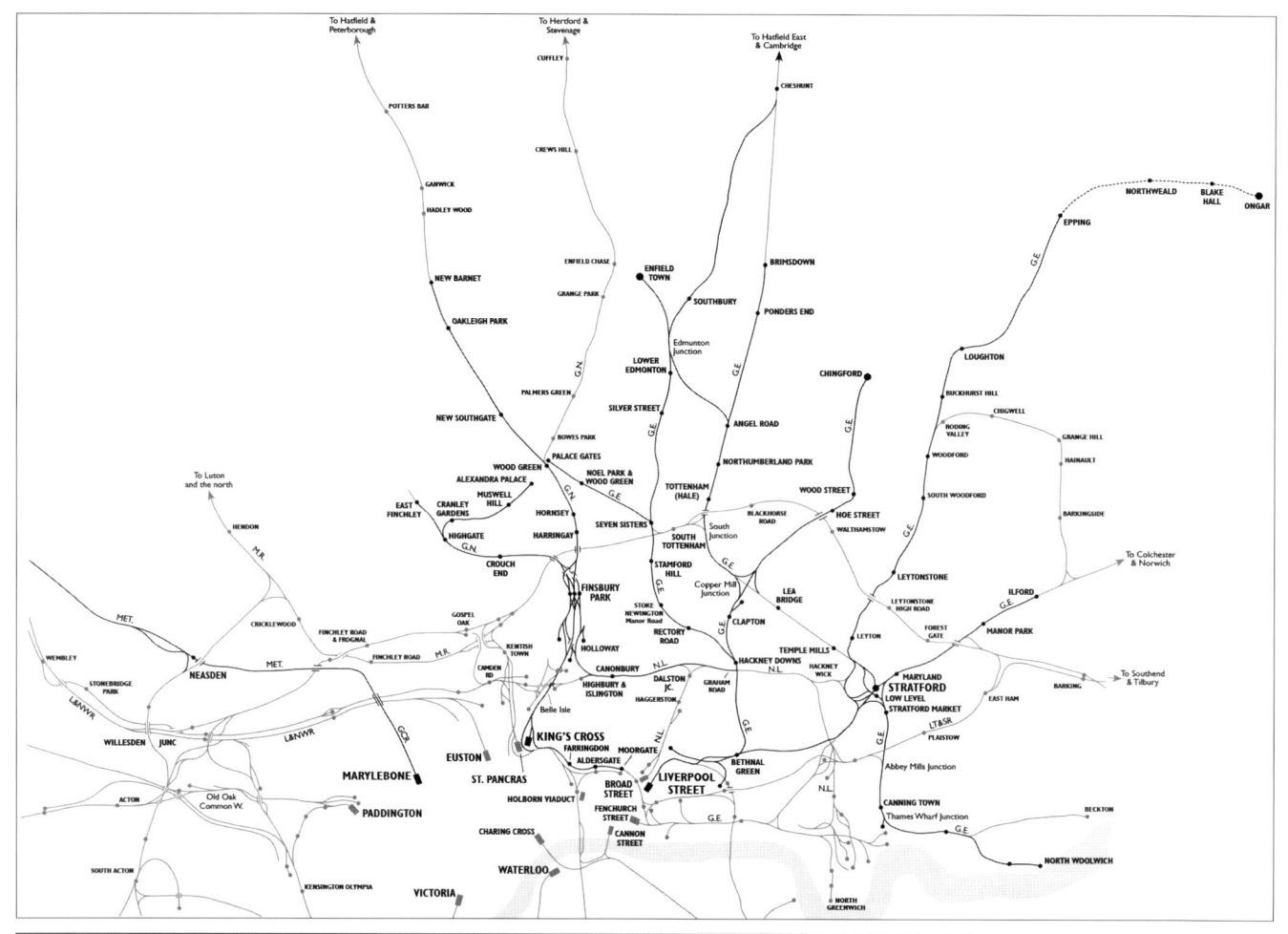

'A4' 4-6-2 No. 60033 *Seagull* is almost ready for departure with 'The Elizabethan' from King's Cross on 5th September 1955. This train was formerly the 'Capitals Limited' until June 1953 when it was renamed following the crowning of Queen Elizabeth II. 'The Elizabethan' ran only during the summer months and only on weekdays, running non-stop over the 393 miles to Edinburgh Waverley.

Introduction and Acknowledgements

This is the twelfth in a series of books, depicting the first 25 years of British Railways, and is the fourth and final part covering the London area. We have been fortunate to have had access to hundreds of different pictures from which to choose the final selection presented here. At an early stage, we made the decision to include photographs spanning the early British Railways era through to the pre-TOPS diesels and electrics, although the emphasis is on that interesting transitional period of the late 1950s and early 1960s.

This volume covers the Eastern Region lines, from the terminus stations at King's Cross, Liverpool Street and Marylebone out along the main lines as far New Barnet, Ilford and Neasden respectively, the Metropolitan Widened Lines between King's Cross and Moorgate and that part of the North London Line from Hackney to Canonbury. It also includes the former Great Eastern Railway branches to North Woolwich, Chingford, Enfield Town, Ongar and Palace Gates, and the ex-Great Northern Railway branch to Alexandra Palace.

We visit the three principal motive power depots serving the former Great Northern Railway lines, King's Cross 'Top Shed', Hornsey and Finsbury Park, the massive complex that was the Great Eastern's Stratford Shed and Works, and the Great Central shed at Neasden. We also take in the freight traffic around the marshalling yards of Ferme Park and Temple Mills.

Express motive power on the main line out of King's Cross was dominated by Pacifics and 'Britannia's shone for a decade on the Great Eastern. The Great Central enjoyed a few years of Gresley Pacifics before a long decline of its express services. All three termini saw extensive commuter traffic with 0-6-2Ts of different, but visually similar, designs employed on the services from King's Cross and Liverpool Street; both employed articulated coaching stock, the former using four-car sets and the latter with five-car sets. For forty years from 1920, the Great Eastern Railway "Jazz" was the most intensive steam-worked suburban operation in the world. The Epping to Ongar line saw ancient 2-4-2Ts operating a push-pull service on behalf of London Transport until it was electrified in 1957, long after similar services to Alexandra Palace and Palace Gates ended. Marylebone's suburban services at nationalisation were worked by 4-6-2Ts but these were replaced by Thompson 'L1' 2-6-4Ts and then by LM&SR Fairburn and BR Standard 2-6-4Ts.

Electrification came to the suburban lines from Liverpool Street in several stages, beginning in 1949 and completed in 1960 when the "Jazz" was replaced by electric multiple units. A mix of DMUs and locomotive-hauled trains took over at King's Cross. Dieselisation of main line services on both the Great Eastern and Great Northern lines began in 1958 and was complete by the end of 1963, whereas those on the Great Central ended in 1966 with run-down ex LM&SR 4-6-0s. King's Cross saw four different Type '2' diesel classes before standardisation on the Brush design. There was a similar result on the Great Eastern as the low-powered and unreliable designs were phased out. By the late 1960s the ubiquitous Brush Type '4' had become the core express motive power, supported on the Great Eastern by the English Electric Type '3' and in second place behind the small but iconic 'Deltic' fleet on the East Coast main line.

As with the previous London volumes, we have included detailed maps with the location of the principal stations and depots showing how they fit into the Capital's streets. Platform layouts are also provided for each of the termini.

Acknowledgements

Our thanks go to Tony Wright for his help with the captions. Any errors remaining are of course entirely the responsibility of the authors. The majority of the pictures in this volume are from the www.Rail-Online.co.uk collection including many from Rail Archive Stephenson. We have taken the opportunity to include a number of whole page portraits which bring out the quality of some of these sixty or seventy-year old photographs.

References

We have consulted a number of books to provide details of locomotives and workings. In particular, the RCTS LNER series and *The Allocation History of BR Diesels & Electrics* have allowed us to include full details of allocations. Books that have been particularly helpful are *London's Termini* and *London's Local Railway* by A.A. Jackson, *Top Shed* by P.N. Townend and the Irwell Press *The Great British Railway Station King's Cross* and the *Book of the Great Northern – The Main Line - Part One*, and the Journal of the Great Eastern Railway Society.

J. Allan
A. Murray

1 – King's Cross

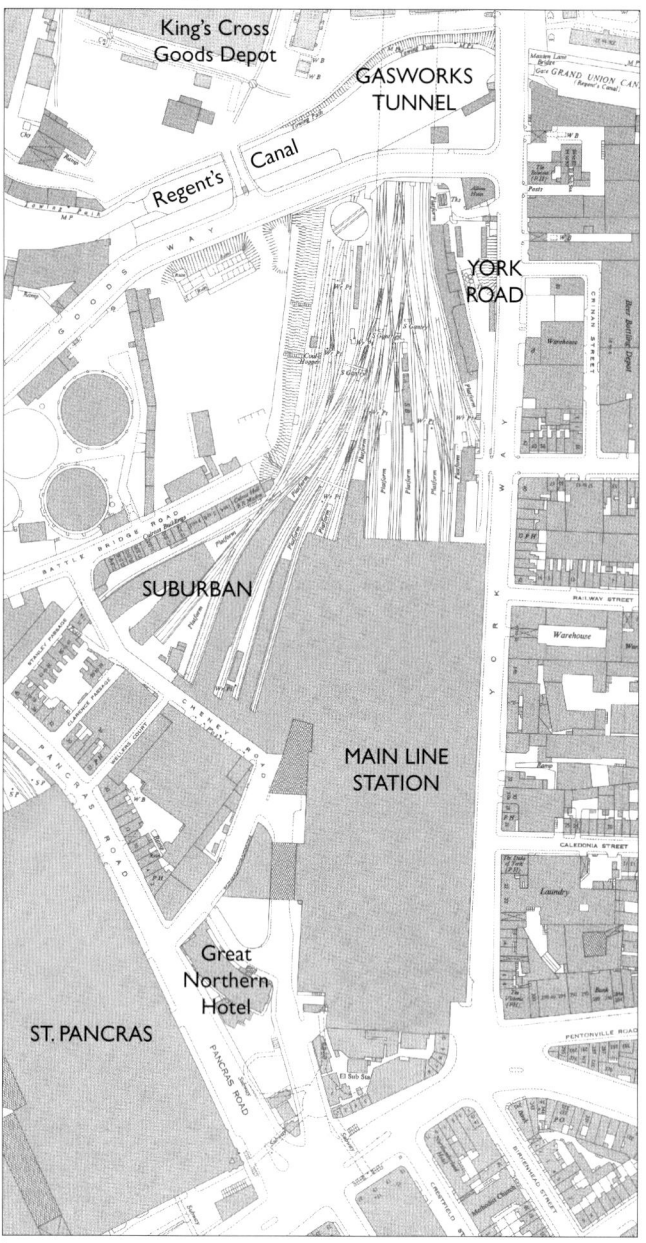

The first station at King's Cross was opened by the GNR in October 1852. It was designed by Lewis Cubitt and had two 800ft long train sheds closed off by a 216ft façade of London stock bricks incorporating two arches with, in the centre, a square 112ft high clock tower.

In 1863 a connection was made through tunnels with the Metropolitan Railway and the York Road platform was opened in the Up direction, Down trains having to reverse back into the main station after emerging from their tunnel. The traffic on the Metropolitan lines increased in 1866 when that line was connected to the LC&DR which generated a large volume of freight traffic to and from South London.

The increasing difficulties of the departure side were remedied in 1875 when three short platform faces and two tracks were added outside the western wall of the main station but a separate platform, known as 'King's Cross Suburban', was not built for the trains coming off the Metropolitan lines up a steep and sharply curved gradient until 1878. Operations were also constrained by the two tunnels on the approach to the station, Gas Works and Copenhagen, and additional bores were built for both between 1877 and 1898.

As traffic continued to increase two additional platforms were built, one on each side of the central wall between the two train sheds. In 1895 another Down local platform was constructed and the locomotive yard was moved to make way for it. The final major changes to the layout were made in 1922-24 to improve the working of local trains terminating at the station but still left the problem of departures blocking inward movements, and this continued until the 1970s. In 1932 an extensive re-signalling of the station area was completed, providing colour light signals and electric point motors throughout.

At the front of the main building a motley collection of buildings, known as the 'village', grew up and despite rationalisation and modernisation it was not until the second decade of the 21st century that the front of the station could be enjoyed in all its original splendour.

The station layout was extensively remodelled in 1977, simplifying the approach tracks after many of the suburban trains were diverted on to the Northern City line into Moorgate. The eastern bores of Gas Works and Copenhagen Tunnels were abandoned as was the Hotel Curve up from the Widened Lines.

At nationalisation, the station was slowly recovering from the ravages of the Second World War and the only change from L&NER days was the appearance of new engines of the Thompson and Peppercorn designs. There was a gradual improvement during the 1950s with speeding up of the principal expresses and in 1958 the first of the main line diesels arrived. After the original proposal in the 1954 Modernisation Plan to electrify the East Coast main line was dropped, twenty-two English Electric 'Deltic's were introduced in 1961/2 to plug the gap and restore the pre-war timings. They held sway until the High-Speed Trains arrived in 1978 before they too gave way to the long-delayed electrification in the early 1990s. The suburban services which were dieselised from 1959 had been electrified in 1976.

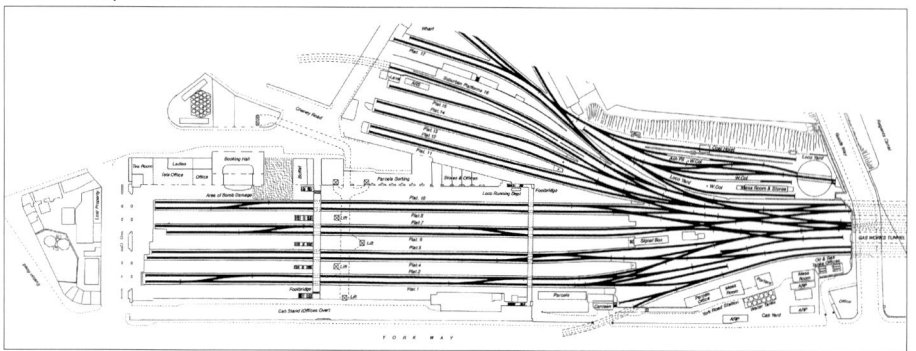

Location map in 1953.

The track plan from c1943. Note there is no Platform 3 or 9, both had been removed in the 1930s modernisation. In the 1970s, the eight Platforms 1-10 were renumbered as 1-8 and Platforms 11-17 became 9-14. Today, the main line platforms are numbered continuously from 0 to 8 and the suburban platforms 9-11, with Platform 9¾ only appearing in J.K Rowling's Harry Potter books.

A 1950s view of the station frontage showing the extent of the 'village' of small shops, huts and snack bars. Between them and the brick façade is the canopy which sheltered vehicles while unloading their passengers.

The Station

The front of the station at ground level on 23rd June 1949 with a variety of establishments ranging from snack bars to chemists. Notice the advertisement for Melbray pies, supplied from a bakery in Fulham run by John Jacks Ltd who were caterers, cafe proprietors and confectioners. A trolley bus runs along an almost deserted Euston Road on route 639 from Hampstead to Moorgate, one of nine routes which served King's Cross. The Traffic 'bobby' on duty has a far from onerous task. A couple of the cars have distict 'American' styling. Note the Great Northern lettering still visible on the brickwork of the façade behind and between the BRITISH RAILWAYS lettering. The four-sided clock in the central tower was exhibited at the Great Exhibition of 1851 and had dials 9ft in diameter. It was the only public striking clock installed at a railway terminus, but its three bells were silenced in 1927.

By the early 1970s the façade was looking slightly smarter and the large lettering had gone, with instead the British Rail Corporate style on the new retail space which had replaced the 'village' in the mid-1960s. The overall drabness is matched only by the awful 1970s cars, with the exception of the taxi and the 'Mini' in the foreground.

Left: King's Cross, viewed from St. Pancras in 1957. Apart from the demise of the trolley buses little had changed in the first decade after nationalisation.
Ben Brooksbank

'A1/1' 4-6-2 No. 60113 emerges from Gas Works Tunnel in April 1961. Edward Thompson's choice of Sir Nigel Gresley's pioneer Pacific *Great Northern* to be rebuilt in 1945 was an unpopular one amongst enthusiasts and the engine was an early withdrawal, in November 1962. A new 'Deltic' is just visible in the diesel refuelling shed on the left and the York Road platform is on the right. Above the three double track bores of Gas Works Tunnel is Goods Way which ran alongside the Regent's Canal connecting York Road with King's Cross Goods Depot, the southern end of which is just visible above the refuelling shed. The colour light signalling dated from the re-signalling in 1932.

A rare picture of the approach to the platforms at track level taken from the cab of Brush Type '4' No. D1980 as it arrived in July 1967. Three different diesel classes familiar at the station during the 1960s and 1970s are in the background, a Brush Type '2', a 'Deltic' and a Brush Type '4' with the tower from neighbouring St. Pancras to the right of the twin arched roofs. The complex approach trackwork with a profusion of double and single slips changed very little until 1977 when it was greatly simplified as part of the electrification of the suburban services. Whether the 8 mph speed restriction signs were ever obeyed seems unlikely.

CHAPTER 1 - KING'S CROSS

From nationalisation until 1957

'A2' 4-6-2 No. 60533 *Happy Knight* from Leeds Copley Hill arrives with the 'Yorkshire Pullman' in 1948. It was built in April of that year and is in L&NER apple green livery but with British Railways lettering and numbers, which it kept until the end of 1949. *C.R.L. Coles/Rail Archive Stephenson*

Left: Spotters crowd the platform end as 'B1' 4-6-0 No. 61089, also in apple green livery, waits to leave with a Hitchin train in 1948. The 'B1' was built by the North British Locomotive Company and entered service in October 1946, allocated to Sheffield Darnall, and received its BR number in March 1948. *C.R.L. Coles/Rail Archive Stephenson*

Peppercorn 'A1' 4-6-2 No. 60120, not yet named *Kittiwake*, gleams under the lights after arrival with the 'Queen of Scots' Pullman in 1949. It had entered service allocated to King's Cross shed in December 1948 and ran un-named until May 1950. It has a plain rimless chimney and snaphead rivets on the cab and tender which were a feature of the 'A1's built at Doncaster. *C.R.L. Coles/Rail Archive Stephenson*

Haymarket allocated Gresley 'A4' Pacific No. 60009 *Union of South Africa* in blue livery ready for departure with 'The Capitals Limited' to Edinburgh on 5th September 1951. This was the summer-only relief to the 'Flying Scotsman' introduced in 1949 which left half an hour before the main train and ran non-stop to Edinburgh Waverley. The title was dropped after the 1952 season and the service renamed as 'The Elizabethan' in June 1953 following the accession to the throne of Queen Elizabeth II.

'A2/1' 4-6-2 No. 60508 *Duke of Rothesay* from New England shed departs from Platform 5 with the 10.5am express to Edinburgh as 'B17/1' 4-6-0 No. 61625 *Raby Castle* arrives with a slow from Cambridge on 23rd May 1952. The four 'A2/1's were built at Darlington in place of the final four 'V2' 2-6-2s and used the 'V2' boilers, producing a Pacific which was a development of the 'A2/2' rebuilt 'P2' 2-8-2s. No. 61625 was also built at Darlington, in February 1931, and was allocated to Cambridge from June 1948 until June 1953.
C.R.L. Coles/Rail Archive Stephenson

Plenty of schoolboy 'spotters and one schoolgirl watch Grantham 'A1' No. 60149 *Amadis* as it arrives at Platform 6 with an express on 8th August 1953. The 'all-electric' signal box was opened in October 1932, replacing two worn-out mechanical boxes 'East' and 'West' which had a combined total of over 200 levers, with colour signalling and electrically switched turnouts. Has the lad on the left noticed the reversed headboard carried on the middle lamp bracket?
C.R.L. Coles/Rail Archive Stephenson

Peppercorn 'A1' 4-6-2 No. 60148 *Aboyeur* departs with the 'Aberdonian' on 5th July 1953. An 'A3' waits for departure time in Platform 8 and an 'N2' 0-6-2T stands in the Central Spur awaiting an inbound train which it will probably take out as empty stock. There is still a gathering of young spotters at the end of Platform 10 at 7pm in the evening. *Aboyeur* was built by British Railways at Darlington in May 1949 and was allocated to Grantham from September 1951 until October 1953.

'A1' 4-6-2 No. 60125 *Scottish Union* arriving with an Up express in the mid-1950s. It was built at Doncaster in April 1949 and allocated to Grantham from May 1954 until July 1957. Notice once again the reversed headboard carried on the middle lamp bracket. Just in front of the locomotive can be seen the valance of the platform canopy of York Road station. The buildings above this are on York Road and include 'The Belmont', a Charrington's pub now demolished.
Raymond McCarthy/Eddie Johnson Archive

Thompson 'L1' 2-6-4Ts could often be seen on Empty Coaching Stock duties at King's Cross though they seem to have been infrequently photographed in that role. No. 67793 is bringing in Pullman stock in the mid-1950s. It was built by R. Stephenson & Hawthorns in June 1950 and was one of a batch of six allocated to King's Cross which were used on outer suburban services in place of 'B1' 4-6-0s and to move coaching stock in and out of the terminus. No. 67793 and was withdrawn in September 1962 after it had been transferred to Colwick in May of that year. *Raymond McCarthy/Eddie Johnson Archive*

'A3' 4-6-2 No. 60108 *Gay Crusader* in 1955 waits to leave on a Sunday afternoon express to Newcastle. No. 60108 had been transferred from the Great Central shed at Neasden in July for the summer services, returning there in October. Of interest is the white paint just visible on the locomotive's bogie side frames, applied to highlight any cracks or fractures which might occur. This was precautionary action taken following the derailment of 'W1' 4-6-4 No. 60700 at Peterborough on 1st September 1955, attributed to a bogie failure. *P. Kerslake*

Rebuilt from a Gresley 'P2' 2-8-2' in 1944, 'A2/2' 4-6-2 No. 60506 *Wolf of Badenoch* from New England shed brings a semi-fast from Peterborough with a Gresley steel articulated twin at the front into King's Cross in around 1955. When the Gresley conjugated valve gear was replaced with three independent sets of motion, the inside cylinder drove on the leading coupled axle and was located well forward so that the three connecting rods were of equal length and resulted in an ungainly appearance. The large signs added below the signal box windows in the mid-1950s left passengers in no doubt about their location! A 'B1' waits in the Engine Yard, with the men standing in front of it watching the Pacific, as are the two beside the signal box. *K. Field/Rail Archive Stephenson*

Not an 'A4' but 'W1' 4-6-4 No. 60700, which was rebuilt from the experimental 'Hush-Hush' water-tube boilered engine in late 1937. No. 60700 had been transferred from King's Cross to Doncaster in October 1953 and its regular duty was the 10.6am from Doncaster, returning there with the 3.50pm from King's Cross, the train it was almost certainly working on 15th May 1957.

Suburban services

For over thirty years from the mid-1920s, the majority of the suburban services out of King's Cross were worked by Gresley 'N2' 0-6-2Ts with eight-coach trains of 'Quad-Art' stock. These were permanently coupled pairs of articulated four-coach sets, built between 1920 and 1929, which were specially designed for the suburban services to Hatfield, Welwyn and the Hertford line and could seat 648 passengers and another 200-300 more standing. The first 'N2' arrived at King's Cross shed in December 1920 and the allocation was between fifty and sixty up until dieselisation in the late 1950s. They were designed to the maximum dimensions of size and weight to allow them to work into Moorgate over the Metropolitan Widened Lines and were fitted with condensers to turn the exhaust steam into the side tanks when working through the tunnels and with trip cocks required by London Transport to automatically stop the train if it over-ran a signal. 'N2/2' 0-6-2T No. 69523 with up-turned 'Welwyn Garden City' headboard waits in Platform 13 of the suburban station and 'L1' 2-6-4T No. 67749 is in Platform 15 in September 1958. Another 0-6-2T waits in the Milk Dock on the right. No. 69523 was purchased for preservation after withdrawal in September 1962 but none of the 2-6-4Ts escaped the cutters' torch.

An 'L1' 2-6-4T with an outer suburban train to Hitchin or Royston stands in Platform 13 and alongside is BRC&W Co. Type '2' No. D5315 which went new to Hornsey in March 1959 but left for Haymarket in 1960. The BRC&Ws were only on Eastern Region suburban work for a short time, from delivery in 1958/early 1959 until April 1960 when they were all transferred to Scotland.

A Cravens DMU, later Class '105', with Driving Motor Brake Second No. E51297 at the front, is ready to leave on a late evening service to Cambridge on 4th October 1964. Conversion of the suburban services to diesel operation began in late 1958 and was due to be completed in June 1959 but problems with the new diesels, primarily the North British and English Electric Type '2' diesel-electrics, caused steam to continue on some services for another year.

Below: Brush Type '2' No. D5604 snakes its way over the pointwork from Platform 4 with an outer suburban train to Hitchin or Cambridge on 13th May 1966 while a pair of Cravens DMUs starts their descent into the tunnels of the Metropolitan Widened Lines from the York Road platform on the left. Note the strange track layout caused by the cramped nature of the site where part of York Road station was on the Up Slow line, but halfway along the platform it diverged from the Widened Lines to run into Platform 1. Except for three months at Stratford in early 1961, No. D5604 was allocated to Finsbury Park from new in April 1960 until February 1978, when it was transferred to Immingham. *Brian Stephenson*

Freight

Frequent freight trains were an incongruous sight at a major London terminus but King's Cross was the exception. The fireman of 'J50/2' 0-6-0T No. 68903 enjoys the fresh air after his train emerges from the Widened Lines tunnel in 1958. No. 68903 was built in 1915 as 'J51/2' and was rebuilt with a larger diameter boiler to a 'J50' in 1932. Thirty of the class, including No. 68903, were transferred to Hornsey in 1952 for use on the transfer freights to the Southern Region through the Widened Lines tunnels although they were not fitted with condensing gear. The 'N2's were not permitted to work goods train over the Metropolitan Widened Lines due to weight restrictions, and these were worked by 'N1' 0-6-2Ts until the early 1950s and latterly by the 'J50' 0-6-0Ts.

'J50/3' 0-6-0T No. 68950 blasts off the Metropolitan Widened Lines with a goods train from the Southern Region to Hornsey Yard on 23rd August 1960. No. 68950 was one of the class built by the L&NER after it was chosen as a Group Standard design, entering service in August 1926. They incorporated several modifications from the earlier engines including left-hand drive. The van on the left marked 'Ribble Cement' is chalked with its destination, Edinburgh. An 'A2' Pacific stands in the yard, turned and coaled ready for its next working. The building with the curved roof sections on the far left was the BR District Road Motor Repair Depot. *Brian Stephenson*

1960s – steam bows out as diesels take over

No. 60022 *Mallard* alongside the first 'Baby Deltic' No. D5900 as it waits to depart from Kings Cross on 24th August 1960 with a special to Doncaster Works on which the photographer travelled. *Mallard* was allocated to King's Cross shed from April 1948 until withdrawn for preservation in April 1963. No. D5900 had been in service since May 1959 and had already had two changes of power unit and a third would follow the month after this picture was taken. *Brian Stephenson*

A group of railwaymen chew the cud as 'Top Shed' Gresley 'A4' No. 60028 *Walter K. Whigham* arrives with 'The Elizabethan' in August or September 1961. The man sitting in front of the signal box steps has a grandstand view. No. 60028 was allocated to King's Cross from May 1948 until withdrawn in December 1962. The shed shared the working of the 'Elizabethan' with Haymarket and each year two of its 'A4's were specially selected for the duty. It was originally thought that 1960 would be the final year that the train would be steam hauled, but delays in the delivery of the 'Deltic' diesels gave the 'A4's another year on the non-stop turn.

Probably on the same day although there are several carmine and cream coaches in the train, a 'V2' 2-6-2 from Doncaster Carr shed, No. 60857, comes into Platform 8 with an express. No. 60857 was at Doncaster from 1946 until withdrawn in April 1962, except for four months at Grantham in mid-1960 and retained its original cylinders until the end; AWS fittings were added in late 1958. The versatile 2-6-2s were equally at home on an express freight or an express passenger train.

An 'A3' with a coal-railed tender moves out towards Gas Works Tunnel before backing down onto its train in March 1961. An ex-works 'Baby Deltic' stands on the North Engine Spur on the right and on the left is an English Electric Type '4' and the new diesel refuelling shed. The Mobil tank wagons are probably replenishing the storage tanks.

The second of the Great Northern Railway built Gresley Pacifics, No. 60102 *Sir Frederick Banbury* waits for the right-away from Platform 6 in April 1961. No. 60102 was at 'Top Shed' from October 1960 until withdrawn in November 1961. It has a coal-railed tender and a double chimney which was fitted in April 1959, producing a marked improvement in the performance of the older Pacifics in their final years.

'A4' 4-6-2 No. 60025 *Falcon* produces an impressive show of smoke as it departs from Platform 4 on 23rd August 1962 as a 'Deltic' waits in the next platform, numbered 2 because there was no Platform 3 – this had been removed in 1934 when Platform 4 was extended. *Falcon* was a 'Top Shed' engine for most of its life but spent its last few months at New England after the shed closed and steam was banished south of Peterborough from June 1963.

Six 'Britannia' Pacifics, Nos 70036-70041, were transferred from the Great Eastern to Immingham in late 1960, primarily to take over the 'B1' workings on the two Grimsby-King's Cross passenger rosters and the express fish trains. They proved disappointing at first probably because when they arrived, they were not in the best of condition. No. 70040 *Clive of India* pulls out of Platform 6 in March 1963. This was clearly a favourite spot for railwaymen to congregate away from the platforms.

Diesel prototypes

Passengers stream past the English Electric 3,300 bhp diesel-electric prototype Deltic at 4.40pm after its arrival in Platform 7 with the 12.30pm from Hull, which it regularly worked from Doncaster during 1959 and 1960. It spent its early years on the London Midland Region but moved to the Eastern Region in January 1959, a year after a fleet of twenty-two similar machines had been ordered for the East Coast main line.

Deltic stands out against the dull steam era scene – no wonder it was christened the 'Ice-Cream Cart' by contemporary enthusiasts.

CHAPTER 1 - KING'S CROSS

In its second livery of lime green with light brown upper and lower bands and window surrounds, the experimental Brush Co-Co No. D0280 *Falcon* arrives at King's Cross with the 'Master Cutler' Pullman from Sheffield Victoria on 18th June 1962. *Falcon* was developed by Brush as a twin-engined lightweight Type '4' using two Maybach 1,440 bhp engines which were manufactured under licence by one of its fellow companies in the Hawker-Siddeley group. Following acceptance trials and testing it entered service on the Eastern Region in October 1961. After further trials on the Western Region, it returned to the Eastern Region in April 1962 and was used throughout the summer on the 'Master Cutler' and 'Sheffield Pullman' (the Pullman service to and back from Sheffield in the middle of the day), making two return trips daily and clocking up 3,200 miles each week with no reported technical problems. Except for the first Brake Second, all of the Pullman cars are the new Metropolitan-Cammell type, based on the BR Mark 1, built in 1960/61 for the service.
Brian Stephenson

In the original all-over dark green which it kept until overhauled in mid-1965, English Electric's prototype Type '4' Co-Co No. 'DP2' backs in to Platform 6 in 1964. 'DP2' was built in May 1962 using a 'Deltic' bodyshell, bogies and other components powered by a single 2,700 bhp English Electric 16CSVT engine. It had been transferred to the Eastern Region in July 1963 and was included in the 'Deltic' pool where it worked turn and turn about with the 3,300bhp locomotives.

Now in the two-tone 'Deltic' livery following a general overhaul having run 380,000 miles in three years, No. DP2 after arrival in Platform 4 with the 09.25 Bradford-King's Cross on 30th December 1965. Its successful career on the East Coast main line was cut short when it was written off after a high-speed collision with the Cliffe-Uddingston cement train near Thirsk in July 1967. No 'DP2' was fitted with electronic control gear in 1966 and this was tested and refined before fifty locomotives based on it (Class '50') were ordered by British Rail from English Electric. However, they were beset with problems from their electronic systems and they all had to be refurbished in the early 1980s with a much simplified system. Notice the hose pipes in the six-foot used to supply steam heat to the train whilst stood in the platform and coupled up to the locomotives steam heat pipe.

Diesels 1958-1966

The first production main line diesels to arrive on the East Coast main line were the English Electric Type '4' 1-Co-Co-1 diesel-electrics. From the start of the 1958 Winter Timetable five of these were based at Hornsey, Nos D201, D206-D209. They were intensively diagrammed with an average of around 4,500 miles per week rostered, covering the fourteen most important weekday trains, including the new Sheffield Pullmans and the 'Tees-Tyne Pullman'. No. D201 departs with one of these, probably the 'Master Cutler', in September 1958. 'N2/4' 0-6-2T No. 69586 waits in the Engine Yard.

Before the production 'Deltic's entered service from 1961 onwards, English Electric delivered ten Type '2' Bo-Bo diesel-electrics to the Eastern Region as part of British Railways' Pilot Scheme. They had a single Napier Deltic T9-29 engine rated at 1,100 bhp; the main line locomotives had two Napier Deltic T18-25 1,650 bhp engines. No. D5901 backing into Platform 4 on 21st June 1960 was allocated to Hornsey in May 1959. The class was employed on King's Cross suburban duties and empty stock workings but was quickly beset by numerous technical problems, and by mid-1962 only four were left in service, the others having been sent to Stratford for storage where they were joined by the remainder in 1963.

Three very new Brush Type '2' A1A-A1A diesel-electrics in late-1960, a class which would become the mainstay of outer suburban loco-hauled trains, parcels and empty stock workings out of King's Cross for the next two decades. Nos D5639 and D5615 are in the suburban terminal Platforms 11 and 12, while D5607 on the right is in Platform 15. The four-character headcode is not yet in use with two locomotives showing 'C' and the third 'G'.

Ten minutes before the 10.0am departure time, the first of the twenty-two production series 'Deltic' locomotives, No. D9000 *Royal Scots Grey* waits for departure with the 'Flying Scotsman' in 1964 or 1965. The 'gold'-painted fibreglass winged thistle headboard was introduced in March 1964, replacing the plain, steam-style previously used. *Royal Scots Grey* was one of six 'Deltic's preserved and ran on the national network for Virgin Cross Country in revenue-earning service between 1997 and 1999 as well as on enthusiasts' and charter trains which have continued to the current time.

Brush Type '2' No. D5640 in Platform 15 in 1963 alongside a Cravens DMU emerging from the Widened Lines, English Electric Type '4' No. D346 and the still un-named 'Deltic' No. D9016, which became *Gordon Highlander* in August 1964. The two English Electrics are taking their turn to reverse out from the Engine Yard and then go out across the station throat before backing down onto their trains. *Brian Stephenson*

'Baby Deltic' No. D5903 departs with a semi-fast to Cambridge, in 1966. No. D5905 is in the shadows on the left with an Empty Coaching Stock train. All of the class were removed from storage at Stratford in mid-1963 and extensively rebuilt with No. D5903 returning to traffic in September 1964. They were painted in a two-tone livery similar to the 'Deltic's and the nose ends were modified with four-character headcode panels. This work did not cure all of their ills, particularly the radiator problems and the decision was taken in the National Traction Plan to withdraw what were ten non-standard locomotives; No. D5903 was condemned at the end of 1968 and the last one, No. D5909, was taken out of service in March 1971. *Kenneth Field/Rail Archive Stephenson*

The single Napier engine of No. D5907 produces almost as many exhaust fumes as its twin-engined bigger brothers as it leaves Platform 5 with a Cambridge line semi-fast in May 1966. It was only in traffic for four more years after it had been returned to service following rebuilding in July 1964. On the far right are a Brush Type '2' and a Sulzer Type '2'. The line dipping away to the Widened Lines at the end of York Road platform can be clearly seen. *Brian Stephenson*

With the hotch-potch of buildings making up King's Cross Goods Depot in the background above the entrance to Gas Works Tunnel, 'Deltic' No. D9012 *Crepello* arrives with the 07.36 from Bradford during 1966. Brush Type '2' No. D5626 waits in the centre spur and a classmate stands in the north spur.
Brian Stephenson

'Deltic' No. D9013 *The Black Watch* departs from Platform 8 with the 'The Heart of Midlothian' to Edinburgh in May 1966. On the left a DMU is about to drop down onto the Metroplitan Widened Lines and a Brush Type '2' waits in the adjacent engine spur with another one in the shadows at Platform 2. Three more of them are in the right background which is dominated by the massive St. Pancras train shed next door. *Brian Stephenson*

Brush Type '4' Co-Co No. D1974 prepares to leave from Platform 8 with the 15.00 express to Newcastle in late 1965 or early 1966. This was one of the final batch of the 512-strong class, entering service from Crewe Works in November 1965. Under TOPS it became No. 47273 in March 1974 and then No. 47627 in December 1984.
Kenneth Field/Rail Archive Stephenson

British Rail 1968-1975

In an early style of BR blue, the pioneer Class '47' No. 1500 backs down onto its train in Platform 8 on 3rd March 1970. According to the headcode, it had previously worked the 07.00 Bradford-King's Cross earlier in the day. No. 1500 entered service in September 1962 and spent most of its first decade based at Finsbury Park. It became No. 47401 under TOPS in November 1973 and was purchased for preservation after withdrawal in 1992.

The clouds of smoke emanating from Gas Works Tunnel in steam days were replaced by clouds of noxious diesel fumes. In its original green livery with full yellow ends, Class '31' No. 5605 with a Cambridge train in around 1970.

Class '31' Type '2's dominate the scene as 'Deltic' No. 9002 *The King's Own Yorkshire Light Infantry* backs into Platform 8 with No. 5646 on the left in around 1972. 1A02 was the headcode for the 'Hull Pullman'. One of the Brush locomotives is emerging from Gas Works Tunnel on a Class '2' train from Hitchin.

By the end of the 1960s the products of Brush Traction dominated the scene at King's Cross. Class '31' No. D5594 is next to Class '47' No. 1983 on the 16.20 to York, which is already fifteen minutes late, a train introduced with the May 1969-May 1970 Timetable. The Type '2' has an additional top lamp bracket on a piece of transverse iron secured to the handrails.

A Derby built three-car high-density suburban Class '125' DMU with hydraulic transmission leaving for Welwyn Garden City in around 1970. Delivered new to Stratford depot, the sets were built for services along the Lea Valley line from London Liverpool Street into Hertfordshire and Essex and their Rolls Royce 8-cylinder 220 bhp engines were intended to provide similar performance to the EMUs running on the Great Eastern's electrified lines. After the Lea Valley route was electrified, the sets were transferred to Finsbury Park depot in 1969/70 to work on King's Cross suburban services.

In the dull overall blue which replaced the much more suitable banded green livery which it had previously carried, Class '31' No. 5592 takes out a suburban service on 9th April 1972. By this date most of the trains from Moorgate were worked by a Class '31' and five BR standard non-corridor coaches. All of the Class '31's were re-engined with English Electric 1,470 bhp 12SVT engines between 1965 and 1969 because their original Mirlees JVS12T engines were found to be suffering from serious metal fatigue problems.

CHAPTER 1 - KING'S CROSS

Class '55' No. 9018 *Ballymoss* after arrival in Platform 7 with the 08.15 from Newcastle on Saturday 26th August 1972. On the right is No. 9002 *The King's Own Yorkshire Light Infantry*. The passengers on the left are making their way to the suburban platforms. The sign visible above the parcels trolley on Platform 8, formerly Platform 10, advises passengers to bear left for the suburban Platforms 9-14, originally numbered 11-17 until the early 1970s.

The Engine Yard aka 'Passenger Loco'

The Engine Yard avoided the need for engines to run out to 'Top Shed'; they could be oiled, watered, coaled and turned ready for their next working within about two hours. In late 1923 it was moved to a position immediately to the west of the Gas Works Tunnel entrance on a site which had previously been a dock off the Regent's Canal. A 70ft Ransome & Rapier Ltd centrally balanced turntable was commissioned in 1924 for the Gresley Pacifics; before then they had to undertake an 8-mile round trip to use the 65ft table at Hornsey. It was not until 1932 that 'Top Shed' had its 54ft table replaced to allow Pacifics to be turned there. Peppercorn 'A1' 4-6-2 No. 60148 *Aboyeur* on the turntable at King's Cross station in around 1952, after it was repainted in BR green in July of that year. No. 60148 was one of the batch of 'A1's built at Darlington Works which differed from those built at Doncaster having countersunk rather than snap-head rivets on the cab and tender. Its original rimless chimney has been replaced by the much more aesthetically pleasing rimmed pattern. It was built with electric lighting but, as usual, oil lamps have been positioned above them. In September 1951 the Eastern Region decided to concentrate its 'A4's at King's Cross, transferring the 'A1's and 'A3's from there to Grantham, Leeds and Doncaster; *Aboyeur* moved to Grantham. *Rail Archive Stephenson*

A mix of steam and diesel in 1959. On the ashpit siding BRC&W Type '2 No. D5309 is in front of 'A1' Pacific No. 60128 *Bongrace* from Doncaster and an unidentified 'B1' 4-6-0, 'N2/4' 0-6-2T No. 69586 with a Hatfield destination board and behind it another BRC&W Type '2'. In the centre background a third BRC&W locomotive waits with a suburban service. Note the narrow-gauge track on the right of the picture with the coal tubs running alongside the line of almost empty coal wagons – unloading these was a hard manual task although the small Mitchell conveyor at the end of the track was used to lift the coal up to the height needed to tip it into the tenders. There are spare sections of 'portable' sectional track adjacent to the 'V'-skip wagons; these could not be used on the coal lift so were probably for ash disposal.

'Deltic' No. D9009 *Alycidon* on the left with No. D9013 *The Black Watch* moving out of the yard on 5th April 1965. A Brush Type '4' is in the diesel refuelling shed and on the extreme left of the picture is English Electric Type '3' No. D6768, a rare visitor from Thornaby.

2 – Metropolitan Widened Lines

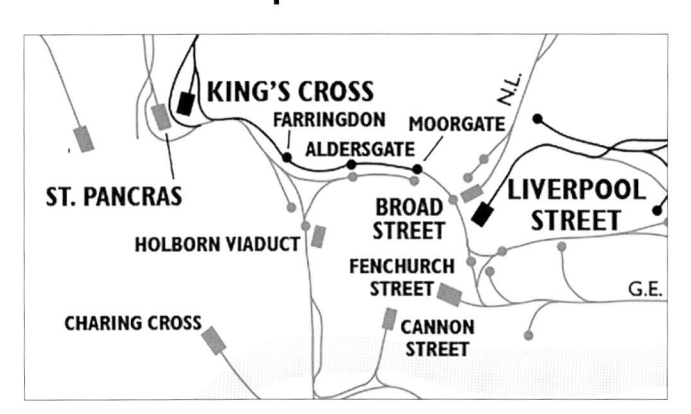

In 1863 the Metropolitan Railway opened between Paddington and Farringdon Steet and was extended to Moorgate in 1865. The Great Northern Railway diverted its local trains from Kings's Cross to Farringdon Street through newly constructed tunnels whose entrances were on either side of the main line station. The York Road platform was opened in the Up direction, but Down trains had to reverse back into the main station after emerging from their tunnel. Goods traffic increased in 1866 when the line was connected to the London Chatham & Dover Railway which generated a large volume of freight traffic to and from South London.

A second pair of tracks, always known as the 'Widened Lines', was provided between King's Cross and Moorgate Street, opening between Farringdon Street and Aldersgate Street in March 1866, extended east to Moorgate Street in July and west to King's Cross on 27th January 1868 for goods and 17th February for passengers. Joint stations with platforms on both the Metropolitan and the 'Widened Lines' were provided at Moorgate Street, Aldersgate Street, Farringdon Street and King's Cross.

By 1869 there were thirty-six Up passenger trains and thirty Down trains using the line and in 1878 the reversal for Down trains was eliminated when the first suburban station was brought into use and the 'King's Cross (Suburban)' platform (York Road) was brought into use for Up trains. By 1893 there were around 100 passenger trains and over seventy goods trains daily each way.

After the First World War, the nature of the suburban traffic changed and competition from the Underground and road transport considerably reduced the need for trains running through to Moorgate and trains only ran in peak hours. Services were suspended between 1940 and 1946 and post-war peak-hour services reduced from nine per hour in 1937 to just three.

Dieselisation on some Moorgate trains began in December 1958, but problems with the new traction, particularly the North British Type '2' diesel-electrics, delayed the full conversion into 1960.

'N2/4' 0-6-2T No. 69572 leaves King's Cross with an empty stock train from Moorgate on 21st April 1953. It was built in 1928 by Hawthorn, Leslie & Co. as L&NER No. 2666. The engines used on the Widened Lines were built with condensing gear and smaller chimneys to conform with the Metropolitan Railway loading gauge. From 1925 they were fitted with trip cocks which triggered the vacuum brakes if the engine passed a red light; this is visible below the footplate in front of the middle driving wheel adjacent to the footstep. 'N2/3' No. 69566 is in Platform 15 on the extreme left of the picture.
R.O. Tuck/Rail Archive Stephenson

The line from Moorgate emerged from a single line tunnel on the sharp, seven chain Hotel Curve into Platform 16 at King's Cross, the gradient of which steepened to 1 in 37 in the platform. This made starting with a heavy train difficult and drivers frequently allowed their engine to roll back before opening the regulator, a process which would often have to be repeated and was made worse by trap points very close to the start of the platform. This was one of the very few instances where a main line platform was on such a steep incline; normally the maximum permitted was 1 in 260. Schoolchildren and commuters wait for 'N2/2' 0-6-2T No. 69535 as it struggles up from the smoky depths of the 'drain' at King's Cross into a crowded Platform 16 with the 2.54pm Moorgate to Hatfield train on Thursday 26th March 1959. No. 69535 was built for the Great Northern Railway by the North British Locomotive Company in March 1921. The suburban Platforms 14 and 15 are on the left. Note the narrow timber planked platform which only just accommodated an eight-coach train. *Brian Stephenson*

'N2/2' No. 69523 leaves Platform 16 at King's Cross with a Moorgate to Hertford North train composed of BR standard stock on 5th May 1959. It was preserved following withdrawal from New England in September 1962 by the Gresley Society Trust and initially went to Harworth Colliery, then to the Keighley & Worth Valley Railway where it appeared in the 'Railway Children' film as the 'Scotch Flyer'. It was moved to the Great Central Railway at Loughborough in May 1975 and returned to traffic after overhaul in 1978. It has been in use there and on other preserved railways since then and is currently (2022) on the North Norfolk Railway. No. 69523 was built by the North British Locomotive Company in February 1921 as GNR No. 1744 and is the only Gresley-designed tank locomotive still in existence. It has right-hand drive, unlike the later L&NER built engines which had left-hand drive, and was allocated to King's Cross from new until May 1962. *W.J. Verden Anderson/Rail Archive Stephenson*

CHAPTER 2 - METROPOLITAN WIDENED LINES

York Road station was between Gas Works Tunnel and the start of the Metropolitan Widened Lines tunnel and was signed as 'King's Cross York Road' in BR days. The line descended quickly down into the tunnel as is evident from this photograph. 'N2/4' 0-6-2T No. 69586 waits in the platform with a train of BR suburban stock on 1st June 1959. A classmate waits in the Centre Spur engine siding to its left, with a 'Broad Street' destination board left on the bunker. No. 69586 was built by Hawthorn, Leslie & Co. in May 1929 as L&NER No. 2680 and was allocated to Hatfield between October 1953 and April 1960; the shed had a small stud of 'N2's from the late 1940s onwards for the through workings to King's Cross and Moorgate.

BR Sulzer Type '2' No. D5054 climbs away from the 'drain' with Empty Coaching Stock from Moorgate to Finsbury Park on 5th July 1963 as 'Deltic' No. D9019 waits to move out of the yard. It went new to March, Cambridgeshire in December 1959 before being transferred to Finsbury Park in January 1961, staying there until the end of 1966 when it moved to Scotland. No. D5054 is fitted with trip-cock equipment for use over the London Transport lines. It became No. 24054 under TOPS and after withdrawal in 1976 it was reactivated into Departmental stock, converted for carriage heating duties and renumbered ADB968008. After spells on the Western Region and then in East Anglia, it was purchased for preservation by the East Lancashire Railway in 1983 and restored to its original number and livery.

Farringdon

The predecessor to the Gresley 'N2' was the Ivatt 'N1' 0-6-2T of which over fifty were built for the Great Northern Railway's London suburban services between 1907 and 1912 and fitted with condensing gear for use over the Widened Lines. From around 1920 many of the class were transferred to the West Riding, displaced by the 'N2's, and those remaining in the South East were used mostly on Empty Coaching Stock duties and on goods trains to South London through the Tunnels. No. 69470 at Farringdon on 2nd October 1955 was working 'The Bernard Shaw Special' from Clapham Junction to Harpenden East and back, stopping to visit the writer's house at Aylot St. Lawrence. 69470 was built in April 1912 and was withdrawn from Hornsey in August 1956, the last of the class there.

'N2/4' 0-6-2T No. 69574 arriving at Farringdon in around 1958. Built by Hawthorn, Leslie for the L&NER in late 1928, it was allocated to King's Cross from before nationalisation until withdrawn in February 1961. The station was originally Farringdon Street, then Farringdon & High Holborn from 1922 and plain Farringdon from 1936.

Aldersgate

'N2/4' 0-6-2T No. 69592 arrives at Aldersgate & Barbican with a Moorgate-Welwyn Garden City train on 13th June 1958. The station was originally Aldersgate Street until 1922 and was changed again to plain Barbican at the end of 1968. Only six of the 'N2's built for the L&NER came from Doncaster Works and the remainder were from three different builders; No. 69592 from the Yorkshire Engine Co. entered service in December 1928 and originally did not have condensing gear but this was fitted in 1932; all of the L&NER built engines had left-hand drive. No. 69592 is in well cared for lined black livery which replaced the wartime plain black that omitted the original red lining. The King's Cross 'N2's had brackets at the front and rear to carry the metal destination boards and each engine was supposed to have a full set of the painted plates; in use these mysteriously disappeared and the man at 'Top Shed' who painted them spent much of his time lettering replacements!

'N2/2' No. 69530 waits at Aldersgate & Barbican with a New Barnet service on 10th June 1959. This was one of the final batch of the Great Northern engines built by the North British Locomotive Co. with right-hand drive, condensing apparatus and short chimney for working over the Widened Lines; it entered service in March 1921. The tracks are curving to avoid Smithfield Market. Note in the foreground the early use of 'zig-zag' weld to build up the running rail surface. This was used to ensure track circuits would operate when 'shorted' by train wheels. It was usually found on infrequently used sections of line where a build up of rust/dirt would otherwise make the correct operation of track detection circuits unreliable.

Moorgate

GNR built 'N2/2' 0-6-2T No. 69529 departs from Moorgate with a Hertford North train in 1949 alongside a London Transport train formed of 'O and P' Stock. The 'N2/2' had been renumbered in June 1948 from 9529, which it only carried for less than two years, having previously been No. 4750 since built in 1921. The lead vehicle of the 'Quad-Art set' is E 86192. The office buildings along Moorgate are in the upper background whilst the bridge carries Moor Lane over the lines. The station was originally named Moorgate Street which lasted until 1924. The station building with its circular tower can be seen above the centre of the bridge. Beyond is the impressive Brittania Building. Today the entire landscape, and street scene, around here has changed with the Barbican development. The building on the extreme left is an electricity sub-station for the Underground.   *RAS Collection*

CHAPTER 2 - METROPOLITAN WIDENED LINES

Moorgate looking to the west from the end of the platforms towards the Milton Street overbridge in around 1950. An 'N2' 0-6-2T waits by the water tank and on the left is LM&SR Fowler '3P' 2-6-2T No. 40022. It was allocated to St. Albans from January 1948 until 1960 and would have been waiting to take a train back there up the Midland main line using the connection mid-way between St. Pancras and Kentish Town which descended on a 1 in 58 gradient into a tunnel below the Regent's Canal and St. Pancras station.

All of the passengers have left for their offices and an unidentified 'N2' 0-6-2T stands in Platform 7 at Moorgate in the 1950s. The class had been used on the Widened Lines trains since 1925, although 'N7' 0-6-2Ts also worked some of the passenger services in the 1920s and early 1930s. Unlike pre-war years when they ran as service trains, the arrivals in Moorgate were worked out as empty stock and then returned empty in the evenings for the Down trains.

The commuters on the opposite platform read their evening newspapers as 'N2/2' No. 69544 arrives at Moorgate on 13th June 1958. One of the large stud of 'N2's at King's Cross shed for three decades, No. 69544 was withdrawn at the end of the year. By 1959 there were four Up trains from Gordon Hill and three each from Hatfield, Hertford North and New Barnet, and in the evening five departures to Hatfield, two to New Barnet and one each to Potters Bar, Welwyn Garden City and Hertford North.

With a 'Gordon Hill' destination board which has been inverted and probably lead to confusion amongst passengers, 'N2/2' 0-6-2T No. 69493 departs from Moorgate on 21st April 1956. This was one of the batch of ten 'N2's built by the Great Northern Railway at Doncaster in 1920/21 and was withdrawn from King's Cross shed in December 1958. By this time the Eastern Region Up trains had reduced to thirteen morning peak-hour services and ten in the Down direction in the evening.
J.F. Davies/Rail Archive Stephenson

Fowler '3P' 2-6-2T No. 40037 from St. Albans shed is ready to depart from Moorgate on 18th August 1959 with the 6.8pm to St. Albans which will join the Midland main line at St. Pauls Road Passenger Junction, just south of Kentish Town. A North British Type '2' diesel-electric waits in the engine bay for the next incoming service. At this date, there were only two morning peak-hour trains from the London Midland Region, one each from St. Albans and Harpenden, and three evening departures, two to St. Albans and one to Harpenden.
K.L. Cook / Rail Archive Stephenson

3 – King's Cross to New Barnet

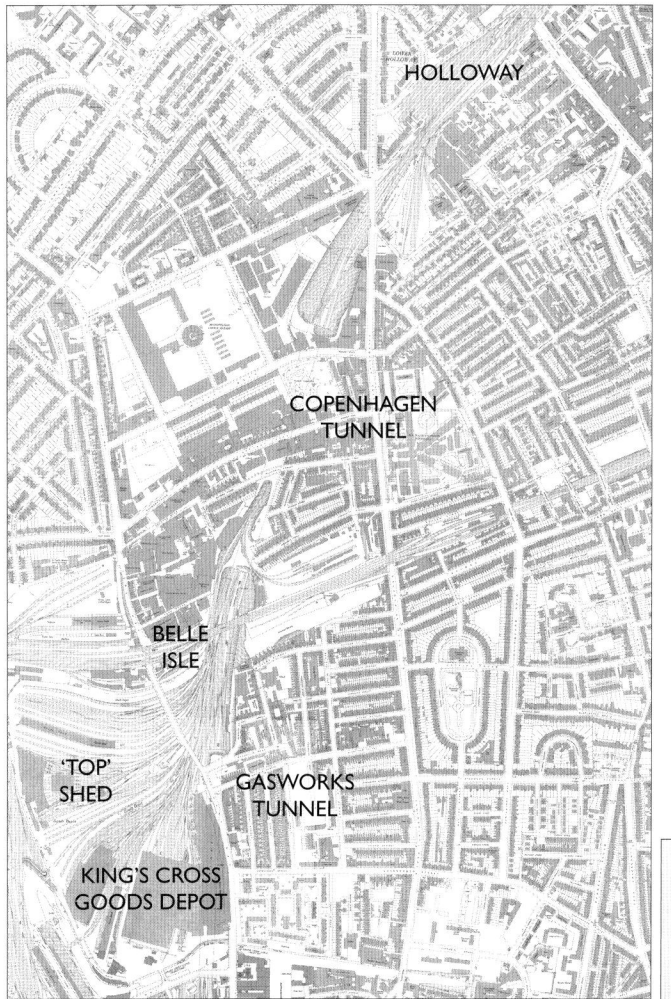

The start from King's Cross was a difficult one for Down trains, beginning with the climb through Gas Works Tunnel followed by more than a mile at 1 in 107 up to Holloway passing through the Copenhagen Tunnel. Gas Works Tunnel had six tracks, three in each direction, reducing to two in each direction by Copenhagen Junction. Immediately after the exit from the Tunnel at Belle Isle were King's Cross 'Top Shed' and King's Cross Goods Depot on the Down side of the main line which resulted in a complex track layout controlled by several signal boxes.

Belle Isle

B17/1' 4-6-0 No. 61640 *Somerleyton Hall* with a Cambridge train at Belle Isle after emerging from Gas Works Tunnel in June 1954. It was built at Darlington in May 1933 and was allocated to Cambridge from January 1947 until withdrawn in November 1958. On the right, an elderly 'J52' or 'J53' 0-6-0T shunts in King's Cross Goods yard; at least two of these were always kept busy there. *D.M.C. Hepburne-Scott/Rail Archive Stephenson*

King's Cross 'A3' 4-6-2 No. 60067 *Ladas* climbs past Belle Isle as it leaves Gas Works Tunnel with the Down 'Norseman' from King's Cross to Tyne Commission Quay on 29th June 1961. It is in pristine condition except for the limescale leaking from a washout plug on the firebox. On the right, 'N2/4' 0-6-2T No. 69568 is backing into King's Cross goods yard. The 0-6-2Ts shared the yard shunting duties with 350bhp diesel shunters after the 0-6-0Ts were withdrawn. On the left are the two Up lines and the Engine line which became the three tracks entering Gas Works Tunnel; York Way overbridge is in the background. *D.M.C. Hepburne-Scott/Rail Archive Stephenson*

'A4' Pacific No. 60031 *Golden Plover* from Haymarket passes under the four tracks of the North London line as it climbs past Belle Isle with the Down 'Elizabethan' on 29th June 1961. The non-stop was allowed 6½ hours for the 392.7 miles to Edinburgh. By this date, six of the new 'Deltic' diesels were in service so this would be the final summer of the A4s working the prestige East Coast main line expresses. Belle Isle Up signal box is on the left beyond the bridge and the three pairs of main line tracks have now reduced to two pairs. To the right of the 'A4' is the 'creep down' into 'Top Shed'.
D.M.C. Hepburne-Scott/Rail Archive Stephenson

CHAPTER 3 - KING'S CROSS TO NEW BARNET 47

'Baby Deltic' Type '2' No. D5901 leaves Copenhagen Tunnel at Belle Isle as it takes Empty Coaching Stock to King's Cross in 1966. No. D5901 was the last of the class to re-enter traffic following refurbishment, in April 1965. Although officially withdrawn from revenue stock in December 1968 it remained in service with the B.R. Research Dept at Derby where it was used in the Derby Tribometer Train until late 1975. It retained its original stock number and was not renumbered into Departmental stock. *K. Field/Rail Archive Stephenson*

A Cambridge to King's Cross off-peak service formed of a Cravens 2-car DMU, later Class '105', with Driving Trailer Composite No. E56427 leading. It has passed through Copenhagen Tunnel on the approach to the terminus in a picture probably taken on the same day as No. D5901 above. It has just passed Copenhagen Junction signal box, the first Down line box north of King's Cross. The Cravens units were used from 1959 on Cambridge, Welwyn Garden City and Hertford North services until electrification in 1977. *K. Field/Rail Archive Stephenson*

The characteristic twin Napier exhausts of Deltic No. D9019 *Royal Highland Fusilier* pollute the air as it climbs past Belle Isle with the Sunday 12.00 King's Cross-Edinburgh on 20th October 1968 while the photographer waits for the appearance of *Flying Scotsman* on an Up special. The tall thin structure in the left centre background is the Post Office Tower with construction work further changing the skyline. *Royal Highland Fusilier* had been repainted into Rail Blue in November 1967 during a General Repair when it was fitted for dual braking, allowing it to operate with both vacuum and air-braked stock. *Brian Stephenson*

Despite British Rail's steam ban introduced in November 1967, No. 4472 *Flying Scotsman* continued under a three-year arrangement previously agreed with BR to operate on the main line, and with an auxiliary tender to augment its water capacity. It has passed under the bridge carrying the North London line and is coasting down the bank past the Goods & Mineral signal box as it approaches Kings Cross with a 'Flying Scotsman Enterprises' special from Leeds in connection with an open day at the Museum of British Transport at Clapham on 20th October 1968. Belle Isle Up signal box is just visible beyond the bridge to the left of the train and in the left background is the 100 feet high Ebonite tower. This was built in 1870 by J. Tylor & Sons Ltd who manufactured water metering and testing equipment and it contained three water tanks at different heights connected to test beds in the factory to calibrate the meters. The Ebonite Container Company took over the factory in the mid-1950s and used the tower as a boiler flue, taking advantage of its height and position to display their name on it; the tower was demolished in 1983, eight years after the Goods & Mineral signal box was closed. *Brian Stephenson*

Copenhagen Tunnel

Blue-liveried Gateshead 'A3' No. 60040 *Cameronian* produces a magnificent smoke display for the camera as it climbs out from Copenhagen Tunnel with the Down 'Norseman' from King's Cross to Tyne Commission Quay in 1950. This was a boat train service introduced by the L&NER in 1931 to connect with ferries to Bergen in Norway. The pre-war title was re-introduced by British Railways in June 1950 and the train ran until September 1966.

F.R.Hebron/RailArchive Stephenson

'V2' 2-6-2 No. 60900 leaves Copenhagen Tunnel with a King's Cross to Leeds express in 1951. It was built at Darlington Works as L&NER No. 4871 in March 1940 and was allocated to King's Cross until January 1953 when it moved to St. Margarets. The building on the left was a warehouse built in 1874 for Mallett, Porter & Dowd Ltd. This achieved notoriety when it was converted to student accommodation for University College London. The interior was gutted leaving only the frontage on Caledonian Road and it won the 2013 Building Design Carbuncle Cup. *F.R. Hebron/Rail Archive Stephenson*

'N2/4' 0-6-2T No. 69575 emerges from Copenhagen Tunnel with Empty Stock from King's Cross in 1952. It was built by Hawthorn, Leslie & Co. in November 1928 and was at King's Cross until September 1961, moving to New England for its final year in service. Scenes from the classic 1955 Ealing comedy, 'The Ladykillers' were filmed here. *F.R. Hebron/Rail Archive Stephenson*

CHAPTER 3 - KING'S CROSS TO NEW BARNET

BRC&W Co Type '2' No. D5312 is about to plunge into the gloom of Copenhagen Tunnel with an Up Hatfield service on 17th June 1959. The tunnel derives its name from nearby Copenhagen Fields, an area which was named after the 17th Century Copenhagen House which stood there until 1855. The first bore was opened in 1850 but to cope with increasing traffic a second was built in 1877 and then a third in 1886 providing three tracks in each direction. No. D5312 had been delivered to Hornsey in January 1959 and would move to the Scottish Region at Haymarket in May 1960.

Holloway

BRC&W Co Type '2' No. D5303 has just emerged from Copenhagen Tunnel on its ascent of Holloway Bank on 27th May 1959 with an Up Hitchin local formed of BR Standard non-corridor stock. The bridge on the left is the Up Goods line flyover; the Down Goods is the line on the right of the picture.

A view from the opposite direction as English Electric Type '4' No. D201 drops down the bank with the Up 'Tees-Tyne Pullman' from Newcastle on 19th June 1959. With the inception of the winter timetables in September 1958, five Type '4's based at Hornsey depot were put on to intensive rosters covering 4,500 miles each week. Fourteen of the most important trains were diesel-hauled every weekday including the Pullmans to Sheffield and Newcastle, and the 'Flying Scotsman' as far as Newcastle. The spire in the distance belonged to St. Mary's on the corner of Caledonian Road and Hillmarton Road, now demolished.

Photographed from the Caledonian Road overbridge, Hornsey 'J50/2' 0-6-0T No. 68931 starts the descent of Holloway bank with a short goods train on 14th June 1954. The Holloway South Down signal box is just visible behind the brake van. No. 68931 was an L&NER built engine, built at Doncaster in February 1924 as No. 3232; it was withdrawn in August 1961. Following trials with various pre-Grouping designs, the 'J50' with the distinctive sloping tank tops which extended to the front of the smokebox was selected as a Group Standard design and examples were built up to 1939.

D.M.C. Hepburne-Scott/Rail Archive Stephenson

'N2/4' 0-6-2T No.69592 slogs its way up the bank with Empty Coaching Stock from King's Cross on 14th June 1954. In the background is the former Caledonian Cattle Market which closed in 1939; the tall building with four chimneys is one of the four pubs which stood at each corner of the Market, this being the White Horse, and on the right is the clock tower which was visible from King's Cross station and still stands today. Note the railwaymen's trackside allotments on the right; these were a feature of wartime Britain and were clearly still well used to grow summer cauliflowers and cabbages.
D.M.C. Hepburne-Scott/Rail Archive Stephenson

'A1' 4-6-2 No. 60149 *Amadis* with a much brisker ascent heading the Down 'Flying Scotsman' has passed under the Caledonian Road bridge, which has two London Transport trolley buses passing over, as it nears the top of the incline on 7th July 1954. *Amadis* was built at Darlington in May 1949 and was already carrying its third livery style starting with L&NER apple green, BR blue in October 1950 and then green in August 1951, the first of the class in this livery. In the first few years its allocation alternated between King's Cross and Grantham where it was based at the date of this picture.

D.M.C. Hepburne-Scott/Rail Archive Stephenson

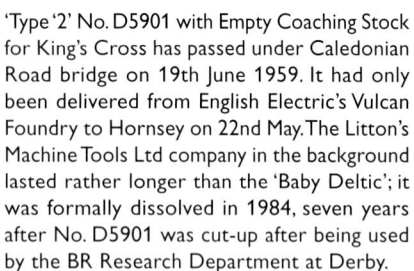

'Type '2' No. D5901 with Empty Coaching Stock for King's Cross has passed under Caledonian Road bridge on 19th June 1959. It had only been delivered from English Electric's Vulcan Foundry to Hornsey on 22nd May. The Litton's Machine Tools Ltd company in the background lasted rather longer than the 'Baby Deltic'; it was formally dissolved in 1984, seven years after No. D5901 was cut-up after being used by the BR Research Department at Derby.

An unusual view taken from the Down Goods flyover slightly further down the bank on 17th September 1959. The Littons Machine Tools Ltd and Caledonian Road bridge are in the distance on the left. English Electric Type '2' No. D5906 is running Light alongside 'N2/2' 0-6-2T No. 69543 heading towards King's Cross with Empty Coaching Stock. The 'Baby Deltic' had been delivered from Vulcan Foundry to Doncaster for Acceptance Trials on 8th May and left for Hornsey on 11th June. Over the next two years, it went to Stratford for a change of power unit on 18th November, then again on 7th March and on 19th July 1960. After a Heavy Intermediate overhaul in December 1960/January 1961 came another power unit change in August 1961. Eventually on 29th July 1963, No. D5906 was taken back to Vulcan Foundry for refurbishment after being in store since November 1962. It returned to service on 29th October 1964 but was withdrawn in September 1968.

Probably on a delivery run from Doncaster after finally completing its Acceptance Tests following a return visit to North British for rectification, No. D6108 comes down Holloway bank on 12th May 1959. The Record Card shows it as built on 14th April 1959. The first ten of the class had 1,000 b.h.p. M.A.N. engines, the remainder were uprated to 1,160 b.h.p. but that did not help their extremely poor performance record. No. D6108 was transferred to the Scottish Region in April 1960 after spending the previous two months in store at Peterborough together with the other nine locomotives.

BTH Type '1' Bo-Bo No. D8231 descends Holloway bank in 1966 with empty stock for King's Cross including two coaches newly repainted in blue/grey. It was transferred from Stratford to Finsbury Park in April 1963. On the right are the remains of the Holloway Cattle Dock which was later used for the King's Cross Motorail terminal and, beyond it, Holloway South Up signal box. *K. Field/Rail Archive Stephenson*

Finsbury Park

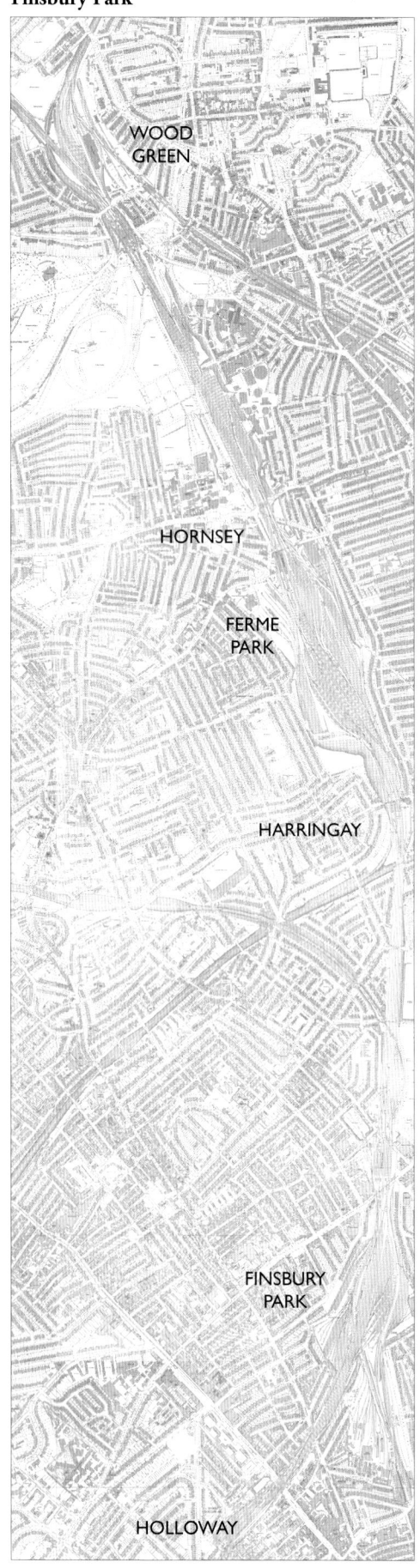

Finsbury Park had eleven signal boxes, seven (numbered) of its own and four independently named. 'A3' Pacific No. 60103 *Flying Scotsman* passes No. 6 signal box which controlled the north end Down side with an Up express in 1960; No. 5 box on the left was in charge of the Up side. *Flying Scotsman* was fitted with a double chimney in January 1959, but did not get trough smoke deflectors until the end of 1961. It was allocated to King's Cross from April 1957 until withdrawn for preservation in January 1963. *Patrick Russell/Rail Archive Stephenson*

Four fairly new Brush Type '2' diesels wait with empty stock in the Finsbury Park Up Carriage Sidings on 29th August 1960. The extensive sidings to the north of the station were used to stable the stock for the inner suburban workings with rakes of both BR Mark 1 suburbans and L&NER 'Quad-Arts' which continued in use well into the diesel era.

CHAPTER 3 - KING'S CROSS TO NEW BARNET

'A1' 4-6-2 No. 60117 *Bois Roussel* has just passed through Finsbury Park station on a Leeds express; an Up express is running through the station. The extensive Up Carriage Sidings on the left were used to stable the stock for inner suburban workings, most of which by this date were of BR design; in the background are a BR Sulzer Type '2' and a Brush Type '2'. Two DMUs stand in the platforms on the far right. The track on the extreme right climbs up to the flyover taking the Down line to East Finchley and Alexandra Palace over the Down Slow No. 2 and the Down Goods line. The two signal boxes in the distance are No. 5 on the right and No. 6 on the left.

Standard 350 bhp diesel-shunter No. D3332, probably running at its maximum permitted speed, on a trip freight approaching Finsbury Park station in the early 1960s. It was built at Darlington Works in January 1957 as No 13332 and moved to King's Cross and then Hornsey later in that year. It was allocated to Finsbury Park in April 1960 and was renumbered to D3332 in May 1961. It was to become 08260 in May 1974. In the left background is the 'Astoria', a very large 1930s-built cinema which became North London's best known music venue in 1971, when it was renamed 'The Rainbow', after having staged concerts since the early 1960s. It was closed in 1981 and lay derelict until 1995 when it was taken over by the Universal Church of the Kingdom of God, a Brazilian Pentecostal church. The United Dairies plant on the right once received traffic by rail on a daily basis from Northallerton in the Yorkshire Dales.

English Electric Type '4' No. D387 rushes through Platform 4 at Finsbury Park with the 7.40am Sunderland-King's Cross on 3rd April 1963. It was one of the later locomotives in the class with four-character headcode panels, built in 1962, and allocated to York until September 1966. The station had two Up island platforms and three on the Down side; note the stylish 'Art Deco' station lighting, a survivor from L&NER days.

On the same day, Brush Type '2' No. D5673 runs through Finsbury Park with an Up suburban service. The code 65 indicated a train running on the route King's Cross or Hitchin to Baldock or Royston, rather than a specific service as used on the longer-distance trains; 2 was for an Ordinary Passenger train and B indicated the King's Cross/Hitchin/Cambridge area. No. D5673 was delivered to Finsbury Park in December 1960 but left for Immingham in March 1967; it was withdrawn in January 1987 following a collision at Maryland near Stratford.

Harringay (West)

King's Cross 'A4' No. 60033 *Seagull* passes under the wrought-iron bridge immediately to the north of Harringay station with the Down 'Capitals Limited' in 1949. The bridge, which was built in 1893, started from Harringay Up Goods signal box at the station and after crossing the running lines descended into Ferme Park yard at the North Down signal box. The bridge's condition deteriorated over the next decade and it was renewed in steel during 1961 and the double track it carried was singled. *Seagull* had been repainted in L&NER Garter blue in December 1947 and received its BR number in April 1948.

F.R. Hebron/Rail Archive Stephenson

'A3' No. 60044 *Melton* on an Up express in 1953 before its transfer in November from Doncaster to the Great Central at Neasden. It had been rebuilt from an 'A1' to an 'A3' in September 1947 and was converted from right-hand to left-hand drive in late 1952. Note the pre-grouping clerestory coach in departmental service in the yard. The now demolished St. Paul's church on Wightman Road stands on the right and to its right the Railway Hotel.

With a fine selection of winter cabbages in the foreground, 'J52/2' 0-6-0ST No. 68831 from King's Cross shed heads towards the station with a Down freight on 15th October 1952. It was built by Sharp, Stewart & Co. for the Great Northern Railway in 1899 and had completed almost sixty years in traffic when withdrawn in January 1959.

Hornsey 'J52/2' 0-6-0ST No. 68808 works through the station towards Ferme Park yard with a trip freight. The 1897 built engine was withdrawn in April 1957.

'N2/2' No. 69555 with an Up freight in the 1950s was built as L&NER No. 2588 by Beyer, Peacock & Co. in May 1925 without condensing apparatus. GER style gear was fitted in 1932 after it was transferred south from Scotland, but it was removed in June 1942. No. 69555 was withdrawn from Hornsey in April 1959. The first seven 16-ton mineral wagons in bauxite are vacuum fitted and fairly new; standard grey unfitted mineral wagons follow behind.

'J50/4' 0-6-0T No. 68990 approaching Harringay West with an Up ECS working. Main line coaching stock was usually worked out to the carriage sidings at Hornsey via the Wood Green flyover, reversing at Bounds Green to reach the sidings which were on the Up side of the main line. The L&NER adopted the Great Northern 'J50' design as a Group Standard and the final fourteen engines built at Gorton were classified 'J50/4'. They had welded tanks and a larger, built-up bunker than the earlier engines, with a hopper-shaped top to clear the cab windows and were fitted with vacuum brakes. No. 68990, built in July 1939, was at Hornsey from November 1952 until withdrawal in April 1961.

'N2/2' 0-6-2T No. 69545 approaching Harringay West with an Up train in the late 1950s. The BR built suburban set is branded 'KING'S CROSS INNER SUB'. The brick arches on the right carry the tracks up to the flyover. A diesel shunter is in the yard to the right of the Ferme Park South Down signal box.

CHAPTER 3 - KING'S CROSS TO NEW BARNET

BR Standard '9F' 2-10-0 No. 92174 from Doncaster shed heads a train of 'Blue Spot' fish empties north through the station on 3rd April 1958. It was built at Crewe in February of that year and had been in service for less than eight years when it was withdrawn in December 1965. Note the train of condemned wooden open wagons in the background keeping company with a Departmental coach. *B.W. Brooksbank*

The first North British Type '2' No. D6100 approaches Harringay with an express to King's Cross on 24th October 1959. The formation of the train suggests it is probably a Cambridge 'Buffet Express'. No. D6100 was delivered new to Hornsey in March 1959 after protracted acceptance tests during which it was returned twice to NBL from Doncaster for 'adjustments'. It was in service for only eleven months before being stored at Peterborough in February 1960 and was then sent packing back to Scotland along with the rest of the Eastern Region members of the class.

Three Cravens two-car DMU sets on their way to the capital at Harringay in around 1960. Note the ballast on the platform and the L&NER cast iron seatback name. The signals on the left controlled the entry into Ferme Park yard. The start of the incline to the flyover is to the right of the DMU.

'Britannia' No. 70038 *Robin Hood* with an Up express approaching Harringay West on 27th June 1962. On the right are Ferme Park Up Sidings and in the distance is Hornsey station. A Sulzer Type '2' diesel is on the recently rebuilt flyover between the Up and Down sides.

CHAPTER 3 - KING'S CROSS TO NEW BARNET

Hornsey and Ferme Park

Looking north from the Hornsey footbridge as Gresley 'J6' 0-6-0 No. 64253 heads a southbound freight on 3rd June 1959. North British Type '2' No. D6107 rests at the back of Hornsey shed between trips with Empty Coaching Stock to King's Cross. It had been completed by North British in March but failed during acceptance tests at Doncaster and was returned to Glasgow for rectification. It finally arrived at Hornsey in April. The Up Carriage Sidings in the distance are full of main line stock. In the centre of the view is the Hornsey Gas Works, which were built on this site from 1884 onwards by the Hornsey Gas Company. The works were served by two sidings via wagon turntables. In 1949 the works passed to the North Thames Gas Board but it was closed in 1957.

The first 'V2' 2-6-2 No. 60800 *Green Arrow* doing what it was designed for, probably on the 2pm Scotch Goods from King's Cross in 1958. It was preserved in the National Collection after withdrawal in August 1962 and worked on the main line between 1973 and 2008 and then it became a static exhibit at the National Railway Museum. *Green Arrow* was placed on loan to the Rail Heritage Centre at the Danum Gallery in Doncaster which opened in September 2021. There are a couple of 'P'-series ex-private owner coal wagons in the siding, along with the 16-ton steel minerals built to replace the old wooden-bodied wagons.

Peppercorn 'A1' No. 60142 *Edward Fletcher* brings a Down express through Hornsey on 12th May 1958. It was allocated to Gateshead from new in February 1949 until September 1960. The long footbridge offered enthusiasts a superb vantage point to watch proceedings on the main line, Ferme Park Up Sidings and the side of Hornsey engine shed. The Up and Down Sidings were opened in 1888 and considerably expanded in the 1890s. The platforms were accessed via the footbridge which came from Tottenham Lane to the right and Hampden Road to the left.

N2/4' No. 69572 approaches Hornsey station with a train for Hertford North made up of BR standard suburban stock on 23rd May 1958. It was built in November 1928 by Hawthorn, Leslie & Co. and was in service until March 1961. Ferme Park North Down box and the Down Sidings are on the right.

CHAPTER 3 - KING'S CROSS TO NEW BARNET

A handful of enthusiasts, one with a camera, are on the platform on New Year's Day 1960 to watch 'A4' No. 60029 *Woodcock* sweep through with a Down express. The water tower and wagons in the background are in Ferme Park Down Sidings. No. 60029 was a 'Top Shed' engine for two decades, from October 1943 until June 1963 and had been fitted with a double chimney in October 1958.

'Top Shed' 'A3' 4-6-2 No. 60061 *Pretty Polly* lives up to its name whilst working the Down 'Yorkshire Pullman' at Hornsey in 1960 as a couple of old railwaymen observe the scene at Hornsey station. There are wing deflectors on either side of the double chimney, fitted in November 1959 but, after trials with four of the class, it was concluded that they were ineffective and from early 1961 trough-type deflectors were used on the 'A3's.

With the sidings of Ferme Park on either side, 'V2' 2-6-2 No. 60902 heads a Down express at Hornsey on 23rd May 1960. No. 60902 was one of the wartime built 'V2's, entering service in March 1940, and was transferred to King's Cross in July 1955. Unsurprisingly, it has retained its original monobloc cast cylinders with the partly hidden steam pipe covers, but it was fitted with a double chimney in October 1961, less than two years before it was withdrawn.

'L1' 2-6-4T No. 67792 with a Down local leaves Hornsey with a trail of smoke on 27th May 1960. It was built in June 1950 by R. Stephenson & Hawthorns and was withdrawn in December 1962, a year after it had been transferred to Colwick from King's Cross. Hornsey Up Goods signal box is on the left.

In another picture taken from the extended footbridge looking north-west, 'N2/4' 0-6-2T No. 69579 pulls a mixed bag of stock out of Hornsey Up Carriage Sidings in 1959 with ex-works Thompson Restaurant Car and companion Open First, followed by a similar pair of Gresley coaches and several full brakes and parcels vans. Two North British Type '2's are on Empty Coaching Stock duty in the Sidings while on the left there are several engines and stock in the Waterworks sidings, so named after the Pumping Station visible behind Hornsey signal box. Notice on the extreme left on the top of the hill the mast and part of the building at Alexandra Palace. The bridge girders visible on either side of the train are where the railway crosses the New River and then Turnpike Lane.

Wood Green

'N2/2' 0-6-2T No. 69538 approaching Wood Green with an Up service formed from two Quad-Art sets in the early 1950s. It was built for the Great Northern Railway by the North British Locomotive Company in April 1921 and was in service until September 1962.

The first 'A4' into service, No. 60014 *Silver Link* approaches Wood Green station with the 4.10pm King's Cross-Peterborough on 2nd May 1953. 'N1' 0-6-2T No. 69465 takes Empty Stock towards the carriage sidings at Hornsey. The 'N1's were displaced from regular London suburban work by the introduction of the 'N2's and those remaining in the area were used mainly on transfer freights and empty coaching stock duties. Hornsey still had twenty-five on its books at the start of 1951 but in that year 'J50' 0-6-0Ts arrived there to take over the transfer work and most were soon transferred away or withdrawn.

Brush Type '2' No. D5592 at Wood Green with an Up Cambridge express on 15th May 1959. The roof-mounted four-character headcode panel, which were fitted to the class starting with No. D5530, is wasted. The station buildings were demolished in 1974 when the track layout was severely rationalised.

'A3' 4-6-2 No. 60046 *Diamond Jubilee* runs through with an Up express on 10th June 1959. It was transferred from Doncaster to Grantham four days after this picture was taken. 'Wood Green Up Box No. 4' is on the right.

'V2' 2-6-2 No. 60862 from 'Top Shed' runs south through Wood Green with a long Class 'D' fitted freight on 10th June 1959. It had been fitted with new cylinders with outside steam pipes in March 1957 but kept its single chimney until October 1961. The station had two footbridges, the nearer one was a public bridge spanning the tracks and the far one had stairs down to the platforms, with entrances at both ends.

'Baby Deltic' No. D5908 at Wood Green with an Up local on 22nd April 1960. It entered service in May 1959 and its Record Card shows five changes of engine before the end of 1960; other members of the class recorded similar changes. It was stored at Stratford from November 1962 until July 1963 when it went to Vulcan Foundry for refurbishment.

A Welwyn Garden City service formed from three pairs of Cravens DMU after leaving Wood Green with a on 20th June 1958. In the background a train of main-line stock is crossing the Enfield (New Line) flyover north of the station. Empty Coaching Stock from King's Cross was brought to Wood Green and worked over the flyover up its 1 in 51 incline to Bowes Park station before reversing back down into Bounds Green Sidings.

Three Cravens two-car DMUs, Class '105' under TOPS, with Driving Trailer Composite No. E56455 leading, form a Down service to Hitchin or Cambridge after leaving Wood Green on 2nd June 1959. In the background, 'N2/2' No. 69541, which was within two months of withdrawal, is crossing on the Enfield (New Line) flyover north of the station. The flyover had been renewed in 1936 replacing the original wrought iron structure.

'N2/2' 0-6-2T No. 69490 passes Wood Green Tunnel Down Box with a suburban train from King's Cross in spring 1956. This was the first of the class, built by the Great Northern Railway in December 1920 as No. 1606, renumbered to 4606 in 1925 and 9490 in 1946, and was in service until July 1959. The Enfield 'New Line' runs across the background with the Great Eastern Railway Palace Gates station behind it. Behind it, the large building is the Bounds Green Carriage Shed. 'Wood Green Tunnel Down Box' was built by Saxby & Farmer in 1886 and as its name implies, only controlled the Down lines and was where the Down Goods joined the Down Slow as shown in the picture of No. 60032 below; it was closed in January 1965.

A. Carpenter/Rail Archive Stephenson

'Top Shed' 'A4' No. 60032 *Gannet* approaches Wood Green tunnel heading north with an express fitted freight on Saturday 3rd August 1957. It may be the famous 2pm Scotch Goods, but the make-up does not quite look right – there is a lightly loaded, fitted tube or pipe wagon and only one container which is sheeted over to protect the load. However, it is the variety of vans that make this a fascinating shot representing all of the 'Big Four' There is a SR Banana Van, BR built 12T vans of both planked and plywood bodies based on the GWR design. The most interesting is probably the Fruit van with louvred upper sides of GWR origin over in the Up sidings. *Gannet* is on the Down slow which has yet to be re-laid in flatbottom rail, unlike the Fast lines. The signals are mostly upgraded GNR lattice posts fitted with L&NER or BR(E) upper quadrant arms, with the exception of the one on the left partially obstructed by a new post probably for a bracket, which is a tubular post design. The bracket in the centre still has its GNR ball and spike finials. With its semi-detached houses and Art Deco flats and the vegetation still under control, this is a lovely suburban scene.

New Southgate

'V2' 2-6-2 No. 60867 runs through New Southgate with a Down express on 7th July 1958. It was built at Darlington as No. 4838 in July 1939 and was allocated to New England shed from September 1955 until withdrawn in May 1962, retaining its original monobloc cylinders and single blastpipe.

'Front to Front' 'L1' 2-6-4Ts, No. 67797 bunker-first and No. 67745 the train engine, also on 7th July 1958. The latter was built by the North British Locomotive Co. and the former by R. Stephenson & Hawthorn; both were withdrawn in late 1962. The train was probably the 5.39pm from King's Cross which ran non-stop to Welwyn Garden City and was frequently double-headed because a single 'L1' was found to struggle with the nine-coach train.

Peppercorn 'A1' 4-6-2 No. 60136 *Alcazar* heads an Up express and is just about to pass BR Sulzer Type '2 No. D5082 as it approaches New Southgate station in 1961. *Alcazar* was allocated to Doncaster from April 1959 until withdrawn in May 1963. The bridge carries Friern Barnet Road, now the A109.   *Steve Armitage Archive*

Oakleigh Park

A WD 'Austerity' 2-8-0 in a photograph taken in around 1960 from the footbridge at the north end of Oakleigh Park station with the goods yard on the right.

Peppercorn 'A1' 4-6-2 No. 60156 *Great Central* heading a Down express to Doncaster passes through Oakleigh Park station on 20th August 1962. It was one of five of the class fitted with Timken roller bearings on all axles which improved their mileage between heavy overhauls by around 20% compared with the other engines in the class. No. 60156 had been transferred to Doncaster from King's Cross in April 1959 and was withdrawn in May 1965.

CHAPTER 3 - KING'S CROSS TO NEW BARNET

'A4' No. 60017 *Silver Fox* has just passed through Barnet Tunnel south of Oakleigh Park station with an express to York on 20th August 1962. It was a King's Cross engine for all except the last four months in service. *Silver Fox* achieved a degree of fame as the 'star' of the British Transport Film Unit's 1954 film 'Elizabethan Express'.

The photographer has crossed to the other side of the line to record 'V2' 2-6-2 No. 60821 also on 20th August 1962 with an Ashburton Grove-Blackbridge Siding domestic waste working with seven sheeted L&NER bogie sulphate wagons behind the first two 20T unfitted mineral wagons. No. 60821 was one of the 1937 Darlington-built engines and had been fitted with separate replacement cylinders with outside steam pipes in February 1958, only four years before it was withdrawn in December 1962.

New Barnet

'N2/4' 0-6-2T No. 69582 with an eight-coach Up service formed from two Quad-Art sets waits at New Barnet in the late 1950s. It was built by Hawthorn, Leslie & Co. as L&NER No. 2676 in March 1929 and was allocated to Hatfield until June 1959 when it was transferred to New England.

English Electric Type '4 No. D201 is emitting clouds of steam as it makes an emergency stop at New Barnet in 1959. It was not on fire and it is likely that the steam heating hose connecting it to the first carriage had become uncoupled. No. D201 worked on the East Coast main line until June 1961 when it was transferred to Stratford. It was withdrawn as No. 40001 in July 1984.

4 – Great Northern Line Engine Sheds

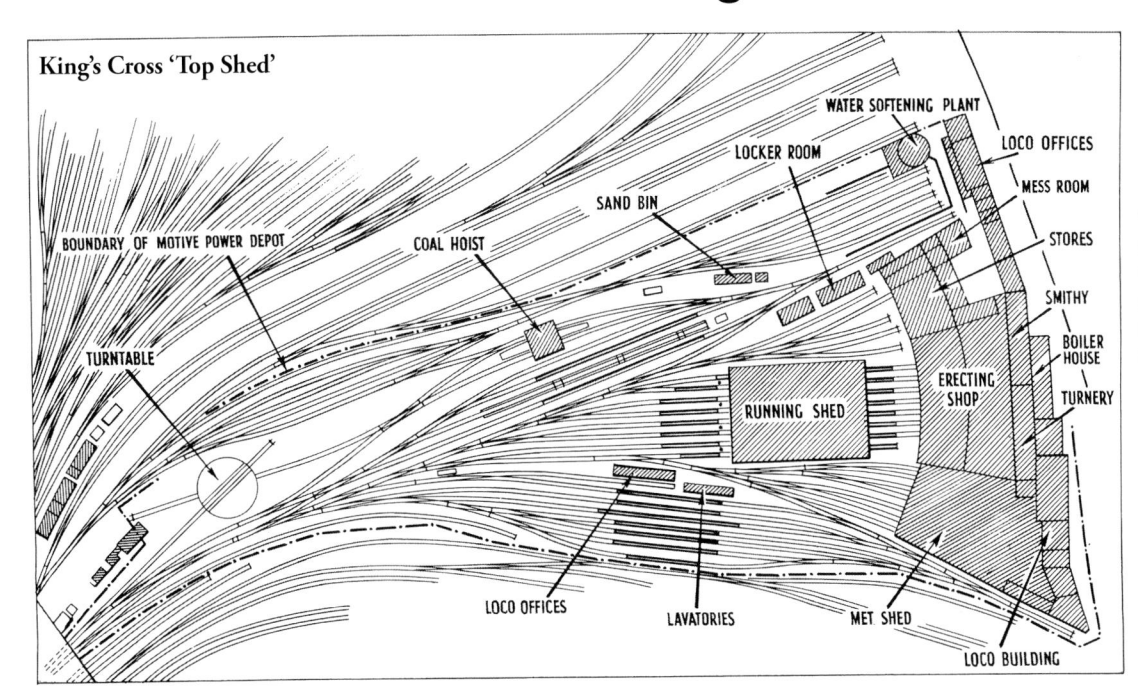

King's Cross 'Top Shed'

The shed layout after the reconstruction in 1931-33 which allowed engines to move easily through each step of the servicing routine.

The first shed was opened in 1850 and underwent numerous changes over the next eighty years as traffic requirements increased. In 1929 the L&NER announced a complete reconstruction of the shed, but some parts of the original buildings survived until closure. The opportunity was taken to provide a much improved layout for sequential servicing. There were only minor changes over the following thirty years.

Under British Railways, the allocation was a mix of large engines, Pacifics and 'V2's, with tank engines for the King's Cross suburban services and for local shunting and freight work.

The shed, which was coded 34A, closed in June 1963 when the ban on steam working south of Peterborough was introduced, although it was some months before it was fully in force.

	August 1950	October 1955	April 1959
'A4' 4-6-2	17	19	19
'A3' 4-6-2	10	2	10
'A1' 4-6-2	12	-	-
'W1' 4-6-4	1	-	-
'V2' 4-6-2	15	10	11
'B1' 4-6-0	10	8	9
'F2' 2-4-2T	1	-	-
'C12' 4-4-2T	2	-	-
'L1' 2-6-4T	4	12	17
'J52' 0-6-0ST	31	17	-
'N2' 0-6-2T	57	58	39
'J50' 0-6-0T	-	1	1
Diesel shunters	8	20	
	160	135	126

'Top Shed' had an overhead water gantry which was capable of delivering 1,000 gallons per minute and was operated by the fireman from the top of the tender or tank. Two Doncaster engines, 'A3' 4-6-2 No. 60066 *Merry Hampton* with 'V2' 60880 to the right, and an 'L1' 2-6-4T to the left fill up their tanks on 17th June 1954.

The 70ft turntable, which was powered by a vacuum motor that was coupled to the locomotive vacuum pipe, dated from 1932 as part of the 1929 depot modernisation scheme; the large cylinder below track level was a vacuum reservoir which allowed an engine which was not vacuum fitted or not in steam to be turned. Note the concrete sleepers leading to the table. One of 'Top Shed's stud of 'A4's, No. 60015 *Quicksilver* is on the table in the late 1950s; it had been fitted with a double chimney in August 1957. By the mid-1950s, although the arrears of maintenance caused by the war had been caught up, the single blastpipe 'A4's were struggling to keep time because, according to Peter Townend the King's Cross Shed Master, the main reason was erratic steaming. His three double chimney 'A4's did not have the same problem and he persuaded the General Manager to authorise the fitting of the Kylchap double chimney to all thirty single chimney 'A4's. This was done in quick time, between May 1957 and November 1958, at a cost of around £200 per engine, and the same improvement was made to the 'A3's which also transformed their performance.

A very new 'Deltic', probably No. D9018, at 'Top Shed' on 21st January 1962 even though the new Finsbury Park depot had been opened almost two years earlier. It is sandwiched between 'A3' 4-6-2 No. 60065 *Knight of Thistle* and an unidentified 'A4' with its streamline casing open for access to the smokebox. An 'N2' and a Departmental vehicle are also visible.

CHAPTER 4 - GREAT NORTHERN LINE ENGINE SHEDS

On the same day as the previous picture, the enthusiasts are armed with cameras rather than spotting books on a shed visit. The number of engines in steam is remarkable at this date with four 'A4's amongst a variety of passenger and freight engines. On the left is the grab crane used for ash removal.

Pacifics predominate in front of the eight-road main line shed on 28th April 1963 with from left to right, 'A4' No. 60025 *Falcon*, 'A1' No. 60150 *Willbrook* and 'A4' No. 60007 *Sir Nigel Gresley*, an unidentified 'V2' 2-6-2 and another 'A3'. A 'Deltic' and a Brush Type '4' standing in front of the 'Met' shed which was the former home of the 'N2' 0-6-2Ts which worked the suburban services, squeeze into the picture on the far right.

Brian Stephenson

Hornsey

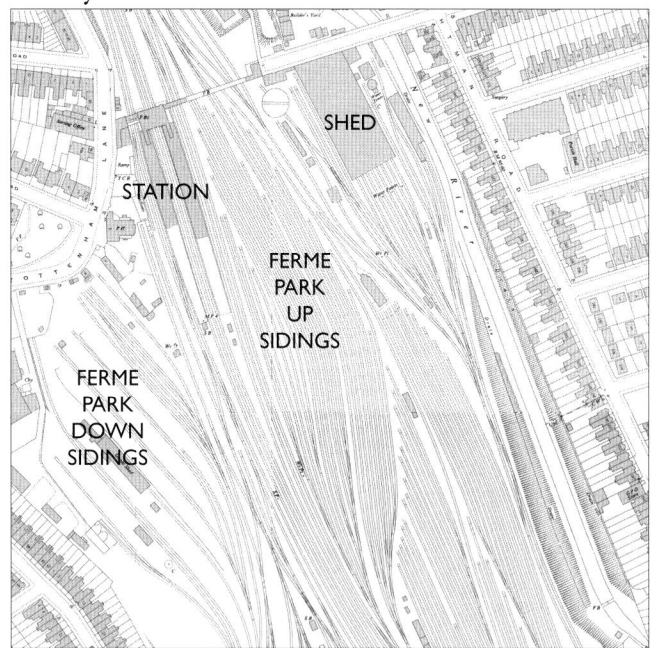

Shed plan in the mid-1950s – on the Up side of the main line by Ferme Park yard.

Hornsey shed, coded 34B, provided motive power for local freight work and shared the suburban passenger traffic with King's Cross shed. It also had turning and maintenance facilities for locomotives bringing freight trains from the north to the Ferme Park Yard, the sidings of which were to the south of the shed.

The eight-road, dead-end brick built shed dated from 1899 and was modernised by the L&NER in the 1920s with a mechanical coaling plant and a larger turntable. Hornsey closed to steam in July 1961, probably much to the relief of the residents alongside in nearby Wightman Road whose protests in 1950 led to a BR investigation of the problem and a four-point plan to reduce emissions. The shed continued as a stabling point for diesels until the early 1970s.

The only tender engines on its books during the 1950s were five 'J6' 0-6-0s, used for transfer freights to Feltham and local trip working. The older tank 'N1' and 'J52' classes were almost completely replaced by 'J50's in the early 1950s. Four of the Great Eastern design 'N7' 0-6-2Ts were used on ECS duties in the late 1950s.

	January 1950	January 1957
'J6' 0-6-0	5	5
'C12' 4-4-2T	1	-
'N1' 0-6-2T	20	2
'N2' 0-6-2T	10	14
'N7' 0-6-2T	-	4
'J50' 0-6-0T	-	32
'J52' 0-6-0ST	34	4
LMS design diesel shunters	-	4
	70	65

In late 1952 thirty 'J50' 0-6-0Ts were transferred to Hornsey primarily to work transfer freights to the Southern Region via the Metropolitan Widened Lines and also to Temple Mills. They replaced the ageing Ivatt 'N1' 0-6-2Ts and 'J52' 0-6-0STs. Three of them are in this picture, taken on 31st March 1954, together with three 'N1' and 'N2' 0-6-2Ts and various freight engines. The original northlight shed which had been refurbished in 1921 had to be replaced in 1955.

Two of the shed's 'J50' 0-6-0Ts, Nos 68907 and 68982 over the pits on 18th February 1959. The former had been built by the Great Northern Railway as a Class 'J23' in 1915 and was rebuilt to a 'J50/2' with a larger boiler in 1932, whereas the latter was one of the L&NER Group Standard batch, built at Gorton in December 1938.

No. 68983 at the head of four of Hornsey's 'J50's lined up in front of three 'N2' 0-6-2Ts and a 'WD' 2-8-0 on 15th January 1961. This was a Sunday and the engines were being prepared for their duties the following day.

Although Finsbury Park had been opened in April 1960, Hornsey was still used as a stabling point for by diesel traction until 1971, mostly those operating on ECS or freight work. Four BR Sulzer Type '2' Bo-Bos and two BTH Type '1' Bo-Bos were there on 11th February 1962. On the left No. D5067 was allocated to Finsbury Park from March 1961 and to its right No. D5068 arrived at 34G a month later; both left for Scotland in late 1966 and they were both withdrawn from Haymarket in 1972, outliving the last of the BTH locomotives by eighteen months. The new roof with transverse pitches that had replaced the decayed northlight roof in 1955 shows up clearly.

Finsbury Park

The new Finsbury Park depot, coded 34G, which was built on the site of the former Clarence Yard goods depot on the Down side of the main line took over the work on diesel locomotives formerly carried out at Hornsey, which reverted to steam. It was the first depot built by BR solely for diesel locomotive maintenance. The main shed had six tracks each able to accommodate three main line locomotives. The three-level working area allowed easy access to all parts of the locomotive.

The allocation on opening in April 1960 changed within a few years as the number of classes was rationalised and Brush-built locomotives became predominant.

	April 1960	February 1965	January 1968
LMS shunters	5	-	-
Standard shunters	12	31	21
BTH Type '1'	-	7	5
EE Type '1'	13	10	-
'Baby Deltic'	10	10	10
Sulzer Type '2'	-	25	-
BRC&W Type '2'	16	-	-
Brush Type '2'	25	54	49
EE Type '4'	6	-	-
Brush Type '4'	-	48	33
'Deltic' Type '5'	-	9	8
	87	194	126

In February 1965, the depot had twenty-five diagrams for the shunters and 120 for the main-line locomotives; in addition at that date it was responsible for maintaining thirty-four DMU power cars.

Above: English Electric Type '4' No. D248 inside the brand new Finsbury Park depot with Brush Type '2 No. D5609, a 'Baby Deltic' and BRC&W Type '2' No. D5319 on the opening day in April 1960.

The Birmingham Railway Carriage & Wagon Company 2,750bhp prototype No. D0260 *Lion* at Finsbury Park in late 1963 showing its impractical white livery. *Lion* was a collaborative venture with Brush Traction and A.E.I. It was transferred to the Eastern Region in September 1963 after a year of trials and running on the Western Region. *Lion* was used regularly on the 'Yorkshire Pullman' but was taken out of service in January 1964 following a flashover on the main generator, a fault which had already occurred several times. There was also severe leakage from the engine sump and BRC&W, which was in financial difficulties, decided to scrap the locomotive.

Now Class '55' under TOPS, No. D9005 *The Prince of Wales's Own Regiment of Yorkshire* stands outside the depot. The full yellow ends were newly applied during a General overhaul at Doncaster Works in April 1967 and show up the usual dirty Gateshead paintwork.

Class '47' No. D1766 undergoing maintenance on 31st March 1968 with Class '40' No. D282 alongside and another Class '47' behind it. No. D1766 had been transferred to Finsbury Park from Gateshead in late 1967 and had three different numbers under TOPS, 47171 in 1974, 47592 in 1983 and finally 47738 up to withdrawal in 2002.

5 – Finsbury Park-Alexandra Palace/East Finchley

The former GNR branches to Edgware and High Barnet from Finsbury Park retained their freight services until 1964, long after they lost their passenger services to London Transport electric trains at the end of the 1930s. During the 1950s there were nine goods trains in each direction, restricted to a maximum of fourteen loaded wagons.

The Great Northern line from Highgate to Alexandra Palace opened with the Palace in 1873 and over the ensuing years its fortunes varied with those of the Palace. In the early 20th century housing development resulted in a frequent commuter service into the City. However, this did not last due to increasing competition from buses.

By the late 1930s there were plans to electrify the branch for use by London Transport trains but these were curtailed by the outbreak of war in 1939. It never recovered and through trains to London were withdrawn before the remaining peak-hour push-pull passenger services from Finsbury Park ended in July 1954; a small amount of freight traffic continued until 1958.

Crouch End

Still with its Hatfield destination board, 'N2/2' 0-6-2T No. 69526 passes Crouch End with a goods train in June 1954. It was built by the North British Locomotive Company for the Great Northern Railway in March 1921 and was withdrawn from King's Cross shed in August 1959.
C.R.L. Coles/Rail Archive Stephenson

East Finchley

BTH/Paxman Type '1' 800hp Bo-Bo No. D8241 on a short freight from Finsbury Park passes through East Finchley station just before 10.0am on 6th April 1962. No. D8241 was built in February 1961 and allocated to Finsbury Park where it remained until April 1963 when it was moved to Stratford; it was taken out of service in April 1968. The third and fourth rail for the London Transport electric service dated from July 1939. Freight trains had to fit in between tube trains and were restricted to 20mph and a maximum of fourteen loaded wagons to operate safely under the signalling arrangements for the electric trains.

Cranley Gardens

Cranley Gardens was opened in 1902 in response to the urbanisation of the area. Driving coach No E86880E, lettered as 'ALEXANDRA PALACE PUSH & PULL', is leading 'N7/3' 0-6-2T No. 69692 as it approaches the station from Alexandra Palace on 25th June 1953. No. 69692 was one of five 'N7's fitted with push-pull equipment in 1949 and which were all transferred from Neasden to King's Cross in September 1951 to work the Finsbury Park-Alexandra Palace push-and-pull trains; when first modified they had been allocated to Neasden to work on the Marylebone-Ruislip service and on the Chesham branch.

Muswell Hill

Ivatt 'C12' 4-4-2T No. 67374 leaves Muswell Hill with a train from Finsbury Park to Alexandra Palace in Spring 1951. It was renumbered from No. 7374 in February 1951 and was at King's Cross until June when it moved to South Lynn. The third and fourth rails for the planned electrification of the branch are in place on one track only but would never be commissioned because it was decided that it was not economic to complete the project in the changed post-war conditions.
Rail Archive Stephenson Collection

Alexandra Palace

The 4.20pm from Finsbury Park with 'F2' 2-4-2T No. E7111 after arrival at Alexandra Palace in 1949. It was built by Beyer, Peacock & Co. for the Great Central Railway as No. 783 in April 1898. Push & pull gear was fitted in 1936 and it was transferred from Stratford, where it had previously been used on the Epping-Ongar line, for the Alexandra Palace push & pull service which started in September 1942; E7111 was withdrawn in December 1950 without carrying its allocated BR number 67111.

6 – Marylebone

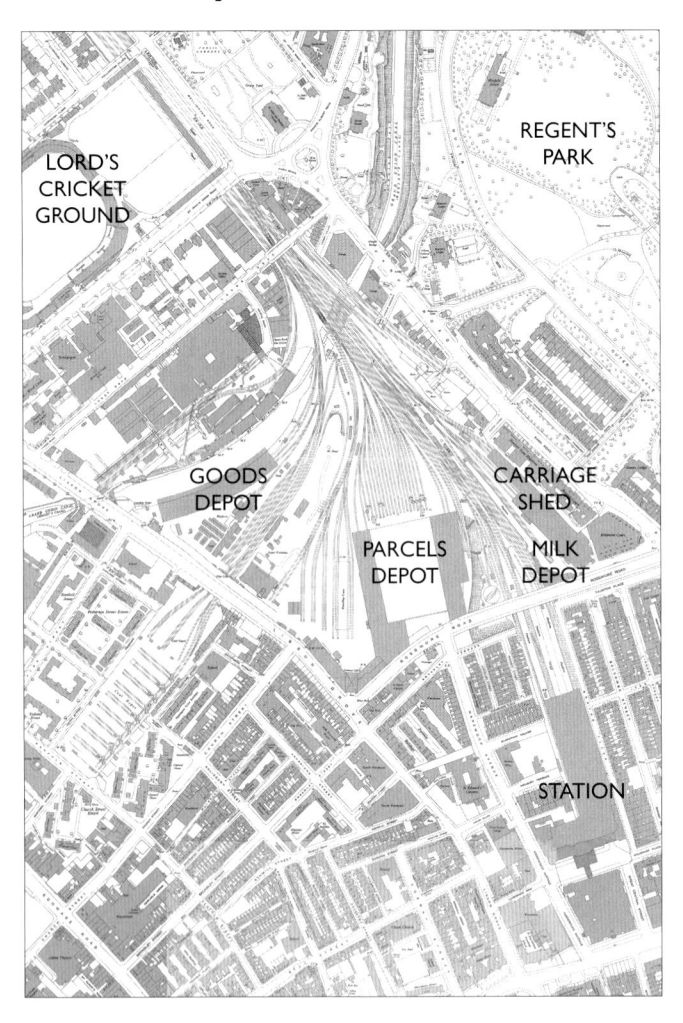

Marylebone station, the last main line terminus built in London, was opened in March 1899 when the Great Central Railway's London extension was completed. Trains ran over the Metropolitan Railway tracks from Harrow until the final two miles into the terminus, built at great expense by the GCR itself. This was because the line passed through the affluent St. Johns Wood area which included the Lords cricket ground, and a large part had to be built in tunnels, and then a fourteen track bridge was constructed to cross over the Regent's Canal.

The station, which was situated on Marylebone Road just to the south west of Regents Park, was a relatively modest affair with only four 950ft long faces covered by an overall roof for about half their length. The ridge type roof had three spans totalling 141ft.

The mix of suburban services and main line trains to Manchester, Nottingham and Sheffield remained virtually unchanged during the L&NER years, apart from the gradual modernisation of the motive power. In 1947 and 1948 two new named main line expresses were introduced, the 'Master Cutler' to Sheffield and the 'South Yorkshireman' to Bradford and in 1949 'A3' Pacifics appeared on the principal expresses. At this date, there were seven Down expresses and six in the Up direction.

However, Marylebone remained a relative backwater and after the London Midland Region took over responsibility for the GCR lines in February 1958 the named services were transferred to other routes, leaving by 1960 only a rump of semi-fast trains to Leicester and Nottingham with just three trains each way daily. These continued to be worked by Colwick ex-L&NER engines but gradually ex-LM&SR types took over, including for a short time run-down 'Royal Scot' 4-6-0s, and ending almost exclusively with Stanier Class '5' 4-6-0s. The Nottingham and Leicester trains lasted until September 1966, leaving only DMUs on the local suburban services. There was a brief re-introduction of express services when re-signalling work at Paddington saw the 'Warship'-hauled Birmingham services diverted there in October and November 1967. The station was proposed for closure in the mid-1980s but fortunately this was averted and it is now the thriving terminus for Chiltern Railways' trains to and from the Midlands.

Below: The track plan from 1899 remained unchanged throughout the steam years. The pair of arrival platforms (1 and 2) were separated from the pair of departure platforms (3 and 4) by a 30ft wide carriage roadway, with vehicles arriving via a steep ramp from the road bridge at the end of the platforms and exiting through an arch at the front of the station.

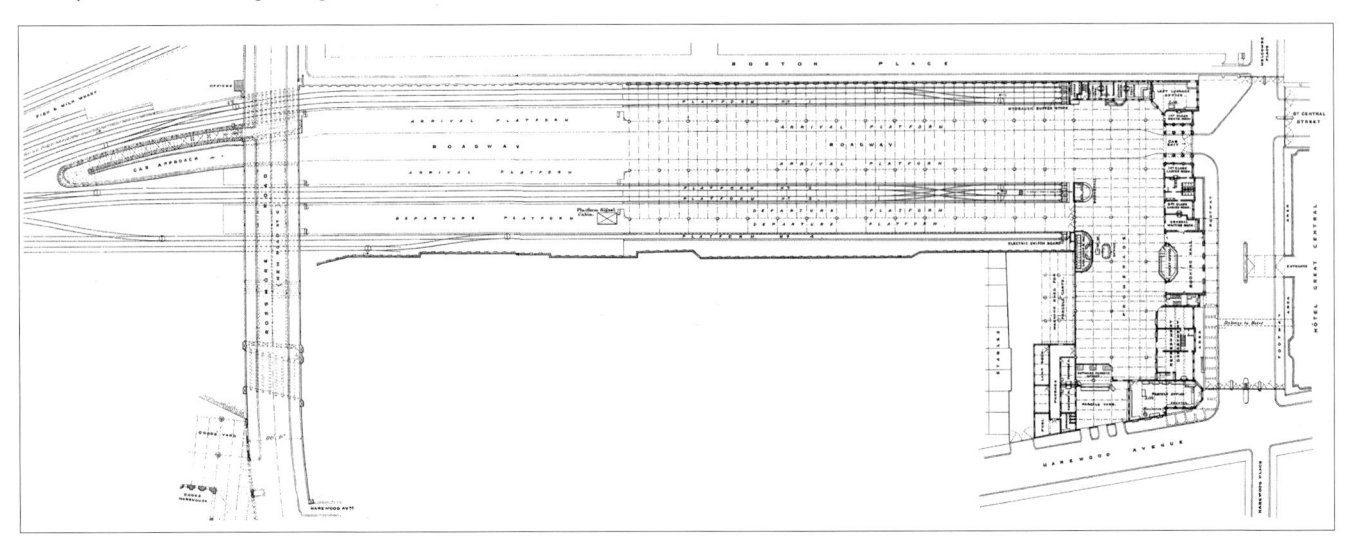

An almost deserted station in October 1966 with two DMUs and a Stanier Class '5' 4-6-0 in Platform 4, from which the longer distance trains usually departed. Marylebone was a large station, somewhat similar to Broad Street from this viewpoint, but only had four platform faces with the centre occupied originally by the taxi cab roadway. The tall building on the right is Melbury House which housed the offices of the British Waterways Board and where British Transport Films were based.

At nationalisation

'B1' 4-6-0 No 1188 departs from Marylebone with the 3.20pm to Manchester Central in 1948. It was built for the L&NER by Vulcan Foundry, entering service in July 1947. Note the six-wheeled milk tanks and a GWR full brake in the sidings on the left which served the Independent Milk Supplies Company bottling plant that was immediately at the end of the station platforms, beyond the Rossmore Road overbridge and is visible above the first coach of the train.

F.R. Hebron / Rail Archive Stephenson

Bulleid 'West Country' Pacific No. 34006 *Bude* approaches Marylebone with the 8.25am express from Manchester Central on 9th June 1948 during the Locomotive Interchange Trials. The Light Pacifics represented the Southern Region in the mixed traffic category and were pitted against the much smaller and less powerful 4-6-0 types from the other Regions. Note the LM&SR tender which was attached because the Southern's tenders did not have water pick-up gear which was needed to top up the tanks on this route. In the background, Marylebone Goods Depot is on the left and an 'N5/2' 0-6-2T is shunting in the sidings on the right.
Colling Turner/Rail Archive Stephenson

From July 1949 all of the High Wycombe and Princes Risborough services were concentrated at Marylebone with a regular interval service of two trains per hour, but this lasted only until January 1951. 'L1' 2-6-4T No. 67715, renumbered from 69014 in May 1948, leaves Marylebone in around 1949. The high-sided bunker held 4½ tons of coal and was stepped to give better visibility when running bunker-first. Neasden had nine of the first production batch of the class and No. 67715 was there from November 1949 until March 1953, moving to Lowestoft when the remaining Neasden engines were transferred to the Norwich District. The 2-6-4Ts could easily handle the Marylebone suburban services but proved heavy on maintenance.

North British built 'B1' 4-6-0 No. 61106 departs from Marylebone in 1949 with the 4.50pm 'South Yorkshireman', the newly nationalised British Railways' first new named train. The title was misleading because, although it called at Sheffield its final destination was Bradford in West Yorkshire! No. 61106 had been transferred from Gorton to Leicester in May of that year. Many of the tanks of milk for the IMS bottling plant were conveyed from Donnington in Shropshire each day, and the working continued until the 1970s. *F.R. Hebron/Rail Archive Stephenson*

Fairburn '4P' 2-6-4T No. 42257, still with LMS markings, sets off with the 6.22pm Marylebone-Brackley in 1949. It was allocated to Plaistow from October 1947 until 1959 and *The Railway Observer* reported that it had been used on Marylebone suburban duties in May 1949, and in the same issue that the service to High Wycombe and Princes Risborough would be improved with a new interval timetable to be introduced from 4th July, so it may have been in connection with this. Ten of the Fairburn engines were transferred to Neasden from the London Tilbury & Southend at Plaistow in 1955 although No. 42257 was not one of them.
F.R. Hebron / Rail Archive Stephenson

1950s

The Great Central Railway Robinson 'A5' 4-6-2Ts replaced the earlier 4-4-2Ts on Marylebone suburban trains from 1911 onwards and were the mainstay of these services for over thirty years until the advent of Thompson 'L1' 2-6-4Ts in 1948. Until then, all thirty of the members of the class built or ordered by the GCR were allocated to Neasden and even when run-down were preferred by some of the Neasden enginemen to the newer engines. No. 69805 was built in 1911 as GCR No. 170 and was at Neasden from July 1950 until June 1954, when the final two 'A5's were transferred away.

Eight Gresley 'A3' Pacifics were transferred to the former Great Central lines in February 1949 and the class was used on its expresses until 1957. The fireman of No. 60063 *Isinglass* chats to the platform-enders prior to departure from Marylebone on 12th May 1956. It arrived at Neasden in February 1953 before transferring to King's Cross in March 1955 and still has a 34A shed plate although it had returned to Neasden three months earlier after a year at 'Top Shed'.

CHAPTER 6 - MARYLEBONE

Gresley 'V2' 2-6-2 No. 60876 waiting to leave Marylebone with the 'Master Cutler' to Sheffield on 6th May 1958. Neasden received nine of the 2-6-2s from King's Cross between 1955 and 1957 to replace its Pacifics; No. 60876 arrived in June 1957 although its stay was brief, and it left for York in November 1958. The 'Master Cutler' was transferred from the Great Central to the Great Northern main line in September 1958, running from King's Cross as an all-Pullman service. Note that Melbury House has yet to be built for the BWB whilst the signal box on the platform is yet to be removed.
T.G. Hepburn / Rail Archive Stephenson

Early 1960s

Fairburn '4P' 2-6-4T No. 42082 arrives at Marylebone on 16th March 1961, probably with a train from Amersham. It had been transferred from Bricklayers Arms in December 1959 and was at Neasden until the end of 1961; there were around twenty of the class there by 1960. The Rossmore Road six span bridge running across the end of the platforms was built to allow for sixteen lines and there was a sharp hairpin bend down a 1 in 20 slope from it which was the original vehicular access to the station.

When KFC did not mean fried chicken! The wicker baskets look to be pigeon baskets so possibly KFC could be a flying club for racing pigeons. For several years after the takeover by the London Midland Region ex-L&NER engines from Colwick continued alongside LM&SR types. 'B1' 4-6-0 No. 61186 departs from a deserted Marylebone in May 1962, just six months before it was withdrawn. It was built by Vulcan Foundry in July 1947 and was transferred to Woodford Halse in September 1957 after five years at Colwick.

DMUs gradually took over the Marylebone suburban services from steam during 1961, and fully from June 1962 following completion of the DMU depot converted from the old carriage shed at Marylebone. A Derby four-car DMU (later Class '115'), one of thirty-five of these sets built in 1960 for these services, departs to High Wycombe on 4th May 1963. A diesel shunter is in the goods yard to the right and further in the distance, beyond the signal box, a steam locomotive is blowing-off in the engine yard. To the left of the main line are the carriage sidings, the carriage washing plant and what was originally described as the Fish & Milk Wharf. The goods yard on the right had four sets of sidings, from left to right were Wall Side and then the Warehouse, the Gentry Sidings, the coal sidings and finally the Stable Sidings whose entrance road is on the lower right edge of the picture. The shunting signals on the extreme right from the coal sidings are unusual with three and four arms on the same post – the exit to the Down Slow involved negotiating three sets of slip points; the first two were to shunting necks. In the right background the three eaves belong to the large Parcels Depot. *M.J. Fox/Rail Archive Stephenson*

A long way away from its early days on the Southern Region when it was one of two 'Britannia's kept in immaculate condition by Stewarts Lane shed for use on the 'Golden Arrow', a grubby No. 70014 *Iron Duke* waits to leave Marylebone with the 4.38pm semi-fast to Nottingham Victoria in 1962. The 'Britannia's were brought in because the duties of the engines which worked the semi-fasts included the heavy overnight mail and sleeper trains which had been temporarily transferred from Euston; they all left when Neasden shed closed in 1962. No. 70014 had been transferred to Neasden in September 1961 and moved to Annesley in June 1962 where it stayed until November 1962.
P.J. Russell/Rail Archive Stephenson

The London Midland Region take over

On 1st February 1958 control of all the former Great Central route between London and Manchester, except for the Sheffield area, passed from the Eastern to the London Midland Region and by 1965 Stanier Class '5' 4-6-0s had a virtual monopoly of the remaining passenger services to Leicester and Nottingham. 44847 from Annesley after arrival at Platform 4 with the 08.15 from Nottingham Victoria on 23rd January 1965. It had been on the Great Central since 1958 and was there until October 1965 when it moved to Kirkby. There are some interesting posters on the right, the film Cleopatra, starring Elizabeth Taylor and Richard Burton, was in its second year at the Dominion Theatre whilst 'The New Face of British Railways' was featured at the Design Centre in Haymarket between the 5th and the 23rd January 1965.

Another Class '5', No. 44858 waits to depart to Nottingham from Platform 4 in mid-1966 during the three months it was allocated to Colwick, from August to November. No. 44858 worked the final train over the Great Central main line into Marylebone on Sunday 4th September 1966.

CHAPTER 6 - MARYLEBONE

Servicing point

One of Neasden's large stud of 'A5' 4-6-2Ts No. 9801 in the engine yard with 'N2/2' 0-6-2T No. 9536 on 21st July 1947. The latter was allocated to Neasden for eight months from November 1946.
J.P. Wilson/ Rail Archive Stephenson

A view taken from the turntable of Stanier Class '5' 4-6-0 No. 44858 in 1966, turned and ready to return to Nottingham. When Neasden shed closed in 1962 this was the only place where engines could be serviced for their return journey. If any serious repairs were needed the engines had to be sent to either Willesden or Cricklewood.

7 – Neasden

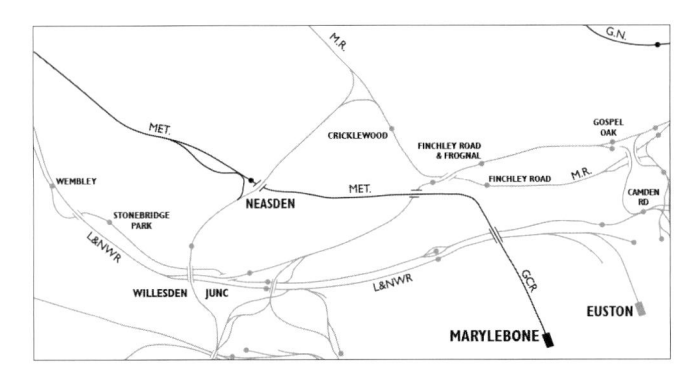

The Metropolitan Railway opened a station at Neasden in 1880 when it was extended from Willesden Green to Harrow-on-the-Hill. The original station building on the road bridge carrying the North Circular Road still exists today. The track layout was considerably enlarged by the coming of the Great Central Railway in 1899, although there were no platforms on the main line, and again in 1914 when the Metropolitan lines were quadrupled. There was a connection to the Midland Railway Brent to Acton Wells Junction line which crossed over the tracks immediately to the east of the station. The Metropolitan established a depot at Neasden in 1882 which maintained both its electric and steam locomotives in addition to tube stock, and the GCR opened its own large running shed servicing passenger, suburban, freight and shunting engines.

Station

'B1' 4-6-0 No. 61137 with an Up express between Neasden and Dollis Hill (London Transport) stations on 2nd May 1959. It was one of the first batch of the class built by the North British Locomotive Co. in 1947 and was transferred from Doncaster to Leicester GC in December 1958. The tall building in the background is Willesden Technical College. Note the limited walkway alongside the retaining wall leading to the provision of recesses should a trackside worker not be able to get to a place of safety.

'V2' 2-6-2 No. 60863 with a Down express passing Neasden station on 4th May 1957. It is on the Fast lines, which did not have platform faces, with the coal yard adjacent to the GC sheds to the right. The bridge carries Neasden Lane and beyond it is the Midland Railway overbridge on the Brent to Acton Wells Junction line. No. 60863 was built in June 1939 as L&NER No. 4834 and was on the GC lines from March 1951 until withdrawn in April 1962, except for four months in mid-1957.

In 1962 a number of 'Royal Scot' 4-6-0s, rendered surplus to requirements by dieselisation on the LMR's Western and Midland Divisions and all in a run-down condition, were transferred to work on the GCR main line services and others arrived over the next year or so; they served out their time until withdrawal and the last ones departed in 1964. No. 46125 *3rd Carabinier* passes Neasden London Transport station with the 2.38pm Marylebone to Nottingham semi-fast as a Bakerloo Line tube train calls at the station on 26th October 1963. Neasden station was built by the Metropolitan Railway in 1880 and was extended from three to five platforms in 1914.
Brian Stephenson

BR Standard '4MT' 2-6-4T No. 80148 passes Neasden South Junction on 13th June 1964 with a train from Feltham at the front of which are empty bogie bolster and plate wagons. In the background, beyond the scrapyard on the site of the former coal yard, is the Midland Railway overbridge on the Brent to Acton Wells Junction line which the train has just left at the junction off picture to the right. No 80148 was built at Brighton Works in November 1956 and was at the shed there until June 1963 when it was transferred to Feltham. It was withdrawn the very next day after this picture was taken!

Main line shed

Neasden was a 6-road straight shed built to the GCR standard design. It was coded 34E at nationalisation and 14D from February 1958 after it came under control of the London Midland Region; the shed closed in June 1962.

Its allocation changed over the years but it always had a high proportion of tank engines – forty-two in 1923, sixty-two in 1948, sixty-seven in 1950 and forty-five in 1959.

Allocation summary

	1948	1950	1959
'A3' 4-6-2	-	3	-
'A5' 4-6-2T	30	5	-
'B1' 4-6-0	9	6	5
'C13' 4-4-2T	3	2	-
'J11' 0-6-0	3	3	-
'L1' 2-6-4T	-	37	-
'L2' 2-6-4T	2	-	-
'L3' 2-6-4T	8	6	-
'M2' 0-6-4T	2	-	-
'N2' 0-6-2T	2	-	-
'N5' 0-6-2T	14	11	3
'N7' 0-6-2T	-	5	-
'Y3' Sentinel	1	1	-
Fairburn 2-6-4T	-	-	19
Stanier 2-6-4T	-	-	9
BR Standard 2-6-4T			10
BR Standard Class '4' 2-6-0			10
Stanier Class '5' 4-6-0			8
Ivatt Class '2' 2-6-2T	-	-	4
	74	79	68

WD 'Austerity' 2-8-0, L&NER Cass 'O7', No. 3056 at Neasden shed on 8th November 1947, a few days after it had been transferred from Colwick to Woodford Halse. It was built by North British in May 1944 as WD No. 70827, loaned to the L&NER in December 1945 and taken into Running Stock following purchase by the L&NER in December 1946, becoming No. 3056 in February 1947 and BR No. 90056 in November 1949. *W. Beckerlegge/Rail Archive Stephenson*

Metropolitan Railway Class 'K' (L&NER 'L2') class 2-6-4 Tank No. 9070 at Neasden in June 1948. Just visible behind is an L&NER 'O7' Class 2-8-0 No. 63188, later to become 'WD' class No. 90509. The 2-6-4Ts were the last engines built for the Metropolitan, coming from Armstrong, Whitworth in 1925, and using government surplus parts produced at Woolwich Arsenal for the design based on Maunsell's 'N' class 2-6-0s. All six were allocated to Neasden and were used almost exclusively on freight work, mainly between Aylesbury and the exchange sidings at Finchley Road. Only two of the class survived into British Railways days, but neither was renumbered before they were withdrawn in October 1948. *Steve Armitage Archive*

Robinson 'C13' 4-4-2T No. 67420 at Neasden shed next to 'L1' 2-6-4T No. 67760 on 30th April 1950 was at Neasden from L&NER days until withdrawn at the end of 1958. Together with Nos 67418 and 67416, it worked the push and pull service between Chesham and Chalfont & Latimer until 1958 after the London Midland Region took over control of the shed and they were replaced by Ivatt Class '2' 2-6-2Ts. Two of them were outstationed at Rickmansworth while the third was at Neasden for maintenance. The futuristic concrete structure on the right is the coaling plant next to the earlier L&NER built one which it replaced because the latter had been built on relatively soft ground which caused problems with its foundations and hence its stability; the 1930s coaler was demolished soon after this picture was taken.

Robinson 'L3' 2-6-4T No. 69064 on shed in around 1951. The class was built at Gorton during the First World War as Great Central Class '1B', (becoming 'L1' under the L&NER until 1945), to haul heavy freight, primarily the coal traffic from the collieries in the East Midlands to Immingham, but their brake-power quickly proved inadequate and they were transferred to less exacting freight work. By 1946, Neasden had no less than fourteen of the twenty engines where they even were pressed into use for special trains to Wembley Stadium as well as regularly working the milk train from Shropshire into Marylebone. No. 69064 was allocated to Neasden from December 1950 until May 1953, when LM&SR Ivatt Class '2' 2-6-0s took over goods workings on the former Metropolitan lines, and was withdrawn in January 1955.

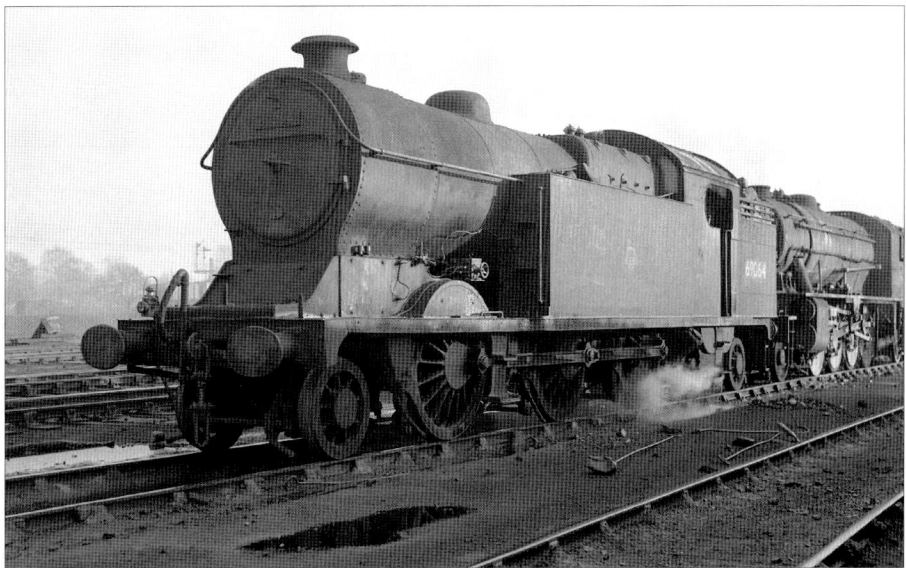

Great Central Railway Parker 'N5/2' 0-6-2T No. 69273 in around 1954. It was built in 1894 by Beyer, Peacock & Co. and was at Neasden from December 1952 until withdrawn in June 1955. The 'N5' tanks were the principal shunting and trip freight engines in the Marylebone/Neasden area and Neasden shed had an allocation of fourteen in 1947, ten of which were still there in 1954.

In 1950 Neasden had thirty-seven 'L1' 2-6-4Ts on its allocation with only five of the thirty 'A5' 4-6-2Ts which had been there two years earlier remaining. No. 67787 was one of the batch built in 1950 by Robert Stephenson & Hawthorns and was allocated to Neasden from March 1953 until September 1958, except for two months at King's Cross in mid-1954. The older L&NER coaling plant has now disappeared.

By the end of 1958 all of the 'L1' 2-6-4Ts had left and Neasden had nineteen of the LM&SR Fairburn design on its books. No. 42251 under the coaling plant on 17th June 1962 had been transferred to Neasden from Plaistow in January 1955 but would move away to Woodford Halse by the end of the month when the shed closed. Behind the coaling tower is the original GCR ramped coaling stage which was retained as support for the 65,000 gallon water tank.

CHAPTER 7 - NEASDEN

BR Standard Class '5' 4-6-0 No. 73156 is coaling up on 28th April 1962. It was built at Doncaster in December 1956 and went immediately to Neasden, staying there until May 1958 and returning in September 1960; it left for the second time in June 1962, moving to Leicester GC shed.

London Transport Neasden depot

Ex-GWR 0-6-0PT No. L98 fills up its tanks at the small steam shed which was part of the large London Transport Neasden depot. A number of the early '57xx' pannier tanks were purchased by London Transport between 1956 and 1963 for use on works trains running on the District and Metropolitan lines after the 'juice' had been switched off at night. The first two, numbered L90 and L91, were direct replacements for a pair of Metropolitan 'F' class 0-6-2Ts. They were repainted in maroon lined livery, with 'LONDON TRANSPORT', underlined, on the tank sides. The panniers were deemed a success and another eleven were purchased, all of the original small-windowed design with single arc cab roof from the '57xx' and '77xx' series. The first two only lasted until 1960 and 1961, but the remainder worked on for some years, with the final three taken out of service in June 1971. Their longevity resulted in six of them being purchased for preservation. No. L98 had been purchased from British Railways in November 1962 and worked for six years when, unlike the classmates withdrawn in the 1970s and saved for preservation, it was scrapped. Built as No. 7739 by the Great Western Railway in January 1930, it was allocated to sheds in South Wales throughout its BR career.

8 – The North London Line

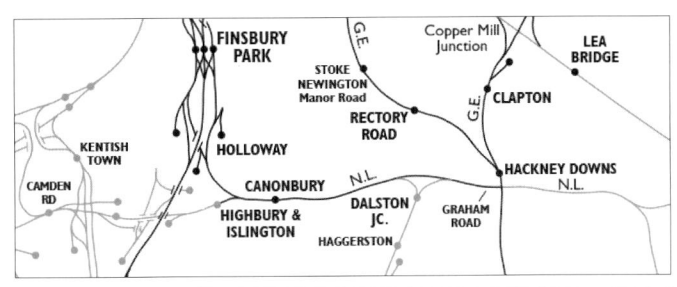

Graham Road

The North London Line provided a route for cross-London freight traffic between the marshalling yards of each of the four Regions situated around the Capital. It had its origins in the East & West India Docks & Birmingham Junction Railway which provided a link for freight traffic from the L&NWR near Camden Town to the Blackwall dockland area at Stepney. The unwieldy name was changed to the North London Railway in January 1853 and a line was completed in 1865 from Kingsland into a new City station at Broad Street, the traffic having quickly outgrown the station shared with the Great Eastern Railway at Fenchurch Street. From 1875 this enabled the Great Northern Railway and its successors to operate a commuter service into the City as an alternative to the busy approaches into King's Cross and the constraints of the Metropolitan Widened Lines.

Graham Road was on the Poplar line which branched off the line coming up from Broad Street at Dalston Junction and went through Hackney, Bow and Bromley to Poplar, and also to Stratford via Hackney Wick. The passenger service ceased in May 1944. The cross-London freight traffic brought engines from three of the 'Big Four' companies to the line; the larger outside cylinder ex-Great Western engines were prohibited because of their greater width over the cylinders. Fowler '4F' 0-6-0 No. 44451 on an west-east transfer freight of Rootes cars passes Graham Road signal box running towards Hackney station on 21st March 1959. It was at Willesden from March 1948 until September 1960. There is great detail for the modeller in the former Great Eastern Railway Graham Road goods depot (connected to the NLR) on the left that was in use until October 1965. Navarino Mansions, built in 1904 by the philanthropic association of the 'Four Per Cent Industrial Dwellings Company' to accommodate 300 Jewish artisans from London's East End, stands on the horizon.
K.L. Cook/Rail Archive Stephenson

The Great Eastern Cambridge main line crossed over the North London Line at Hackney. Hackney Downs station was immediately to the left of the bridge under which a goods train has just passed heading towards Hackney. On the right 'N7/5' 0-6-2T No. 69626 with the 1.54pm Liverpool Street-Chingford meets another 'N7' on the 1.37pm Enfield-Liverpool Street on 21st March 1959.
K.L. Cook/Rail Archive Stephenson

Dalston Junction

'N2/4' 0-6-2T No. 69589 with a Broad Street-Hertford North train approaches Dalston Junction on 12th August 1955. The three 86ft 6in. high co-acting or repeater signals built to be visible above the Forest Road Bridge are very distinctive. The electrified tracks on the right into Platforms 1 and 2 were used by the EMUs operating the Broad Street to Richmond service.   *J.F. Davies/Rail Archive Stephenson*

'N2/2' 0-6-2T No. 69520 arrives at Dalston Junction with a peak hour train from Broad Street on 22nd March 1960. It was allocated to King's Cross until November 1959 when it moved to Hornsey but stayed there for less than two years before leaving for New England in August 1961. Note the very unusual 'restricted space' centre-pivoted lower quadrant starting signals which were of North London Railway origin. The line from Poplar joins on the left and No. 69520 is on the pair of tracks to Dalton Western Junction which used Platforms 3 and 4.

Thompson 'L1' 2-6-4T No. 67768 is ready to depart from Platform 4 at Dalston Junction on 24th March 1960. It was built for British Railways by R. Stephenson & Hawthorn Ltd in October 1949. Based at Neasden, No. 67768 worked on the Great Central suburban services until July 1956 when it moved to King's Cross where it stayed until November 1960. The station, which had six platform faces, had by this date become quite derelict as evidenced by the state of the awnings.

Canonbury

Canonbury was the second station west after Mildmay Park when the North London Railway split at Dalston Junction; the station buildings were demolished in June 1969 and rebuilding was completed in 1970. The mile long link to the Great Northern Railway main line at Finsbury Park, opened in 1874, left the North London Railway shortly after Canonbury and enabled GNR trains to run through from Broad Street to destinations including High Barnet, Barnet, Enfield and Hertford North. 'N2/2' 0-6-2T No. 69512 was working a Broad Street-Hertford North rush-hour only commuter train on 14th July 1958. It was built by the Great Northern Railway in January 1921 as No. 1733, renumbered by the L&NER in 1924 to 4733 and then to 9512 in 1946. No. 69512 was at King's Cross from before nationalisation until transferred to New England in July 1961.

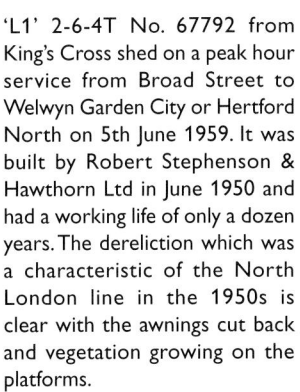

CHAPTER 8 - THE NORTH LONDON LINE

Gresley 'J6' 0-6-0 No. 64233 with a westbound Class 'C' fitted freight heading for the Great Northern main line on 31st August 1958 was built by the Great Northern Railway in 1914 as No. 584, renumbered to 3584 in 1925 and again to 4233 in December 1946 and 64233 in May 1948. It was transferred from Colwick to Hornsey in October 1953 and was there until February 1960 when it went to New England from where it was withdrawn in July 1961. At the front of the train are three Banana Vans followed by insulated meat containers which suggests it had originated at one of the Thames docks.

'L1' 2-6-4T No. 67792 from King's Cross shed on a peak hour service from Broad Street to Welwyn Garden City or Hertford North on 5th June 1959. It was built by Robert Stephenson & Hawthorn Ltd in June 1950 and had a working life of only a dozen years. The dereliction which was a characteristic of the North London line in the 1950s is clear with the awnings cut back and vegetation growing on the platforms.

'J94' 0-6-0ST No. 68073 heading for home at Hornsey with a transfer freight to Ferme Park, probably from Temple Mills, on 2nd May 1959. Canonbury Junction leading to the Great Northern main line at Finsbury Park was only a short distance from the platform ends. No. 68073 was built for the Ministry of Supply by Andrew Barclay & Co. in October 1945 but went immediately into store at the Longmoor military depot because the 0-6-0STs built from June 1945 were no longer required for the war effort. Seventy-five were purchased by the L&NER. No. 68073 was taken into L&NER stock in June 1946; it was fitted with an extended coal bunker in July 1948 and was in service until August 1961.

'J50/3' 0-6-0T No. 68966 with an eastbound freight from Ferme Park to Temple Mills on 13th September 1959. This was one of the L&NER built engines, entering service in December 1926; it was at Hornsey from March 1956 until withdrawn in August 1961.

Highbury & Islington

Pursued by birds, another picture taken a few months later of 'J50/3' 0-6-0T No. 68966 as it passes through Highbury & Islington station with an eastbound train on 5th March 1960. There must have been a surplus of brake vans on the London Midland Region at Willesden as the opportunity has been taken to return two of the Southern Region 'Pillbox' vans to Temple Mills for onwards transmission to Feltham. At least the pigeons seem excited!

9 – Liverpool Street

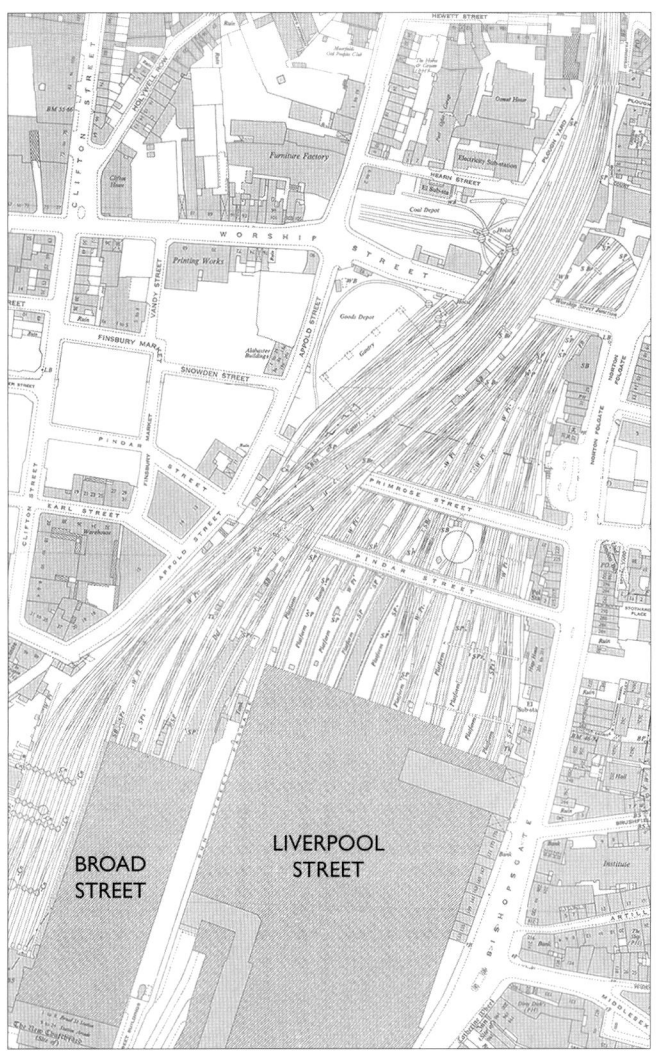

Liverpool Street station, completed in 1875, replaced the original London terminus at Shoreditch built by the Eastern Counties Railway. It had ten platforms, extended to eighteen in 1894 when an additional pair of approach tracks was added. Across the end of the platform area was the Great Eastern Hotel which was built in 1884.

In 1920 the GER undertook a major revision of its suburban services and with electrification financially impossible, a series of improvements was made to track layouts and signalling in the station and on the approaches. At Liverpool Street new engine docks were provided for Platforms 1 to 4 and these changes allowed engines from incoming trains to be moved out for their following departure without fouling the other approach running lines. The revised service was nicknamed the "Jazz" because of the coloured stripes added to the coaches at cantrail level to indicate the class.

Up until nationalisation there were few other changes, confined to minor improvements such as modernisation of the booking office and train indicator boards. On 7th November 1949 all local workings on the Shenfield line were taken over by electric multiple units, completing a scheme started in 1937 by the L&NER which was put on hold during the Second World War. Electric signalling was introduced at the same time covering the station and all the approach tracks.

In 1951 the new BR Standard 'Britannia' Pacifics were introduced and revolutionised the service to Ipswich and Norwich, and they made a similar impact on the Cambridge line services in 1953.

Electrification was extended to the Chelmsford and Southend routes in 1956. In November 1960 the 'Jazz' service became all-electric and an electric service was introduced to Clacton in 1963.

By the end of 1962 all steam workings had been taken over by diesel or electric traction, and over the next decade improvements were made to the passenger facilities and several sidings which were no longer needed were taken out.

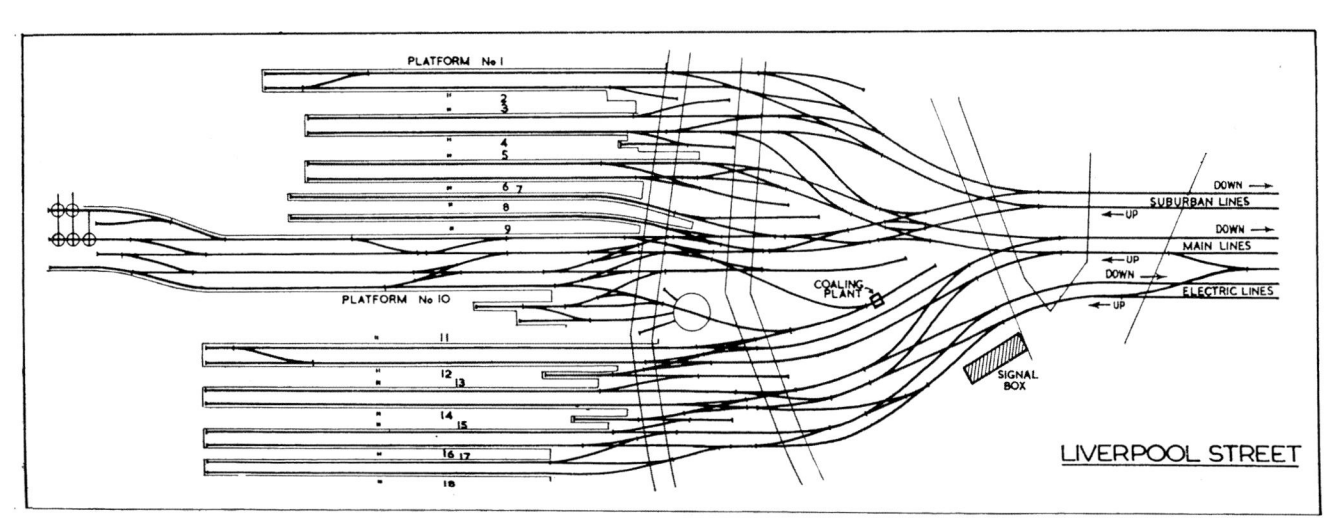

Location map showing the station and the surrounding area in 1953.

The track plan in the 1950s. There were three sets of approach tracks: on the west side were the 'Suburban' lines, the middle pair were known as the 'Main' and the eastern pair the 'Electric' lines; the latter two pairs were swapped over as part of the 1949 electrification project. Although Platforms 11 and 12 were 'wired', they were not normally used by the original electric services.

The station

The entrance to Liverpool Street station, on 15th July 1955, looking northward down the approach ramp from Liverpool Street, showing the awkward entry beside and below the Great Eastern Hotel which is out of picture to the right beyond No. 50 Liverpool Street, the former headquarters of the Great Eastern Railway. The Gothic style tower in the centre background had an imposing clock tower above until it was removed following war damage in 1941. The large building to its left was the old west side suburban booking office which also lost its roof in 1941.

Steam was still very much around in 1958 – an 'L1' 2-6-4T to the left is on an interesting mixed train including an open wagon and a tank – possibly carrying heating/lighting gas – and there is an 'N7' 0-6-2T on station pilot work on the right. Brand new Brush Type '2' No. D5503 standing in Platform 9 was delivered from Brush Traction's Loughborough works on 9th January and was based at Stratford until April 1959. Note the sign on the left which was a feature of the "Jazz" service showing passengers which colour cantrail strip denoted the First and Second class carriages on their train.

Liverpool Street in the early 1970s. The fashions have changed considerably since the 1955 picture! It would have been noisy on this side of the Great Eastern Hotel and the windows facing the platforms must have had to be kept permanently closed to keep out the fumes. The Hotel was completely renovated in 2000 and is now a 5-star luxury 'lifestyle' hotel owned by the Hyatt Group and operates under its Andaz brand. The five-storey red brick building dressed with Portland stone was given Grade II listing on the National Heritage List for England in March 1993.

From nationalisation until 1955

In apple green livery and still with LNER on its tank sides but with its BR number, 'L1' 2-6-4T No. 67702 at Liverpool Street on 16th May 1948. It had entered service from Darlington Works in January 1948 as No. 9001 but was quickly renumbered when it was decided that the class should take the number series beginning with 67701. In the background, at a higher level on the arches, is Broad Street station with Broad Street No. 1 signal box on the right.
J. P. Wilson/Rail Archive Stephenson

A touch of pre-war glamour was brought to the Great Eastern in 1937 when two 'B17' 4-6-0s were given 'A4' style streamlining to work the 'East Anglian' between Liverpool Street and Norwich. No. 61659 entered service in June 1936 as No. 2859 *Norwich City* and was renamed *East Anglian* when streamlined and reclassified as 'B17/5' in September 1937 along with No. 2870. They worked the service until the outbreak of war in September 1939 and were then stored out of use until February 1940. *East Anglian* had been repainted by Stratford Works in April 1948 in unlined black and has large 12in. high BR cab numbers and BRITISH RAILWAYS lettering on the tender; it did not have a smokebox number plate until July 1949. The streamlining was removed from both engines in 1951.

The Permanent Way men pose for the camera as 'Britannia' No. 70010 *Owen Glendower* passes under the No. 8 Primrose Bridge as it departs from Liverpool Street with a Yarmouth express on 3rd September 1951. The new BR Standard Pacifics revolutionised the Great Eastern line expresses. In July 1951 a completely revised, regular interval timetable of fast trains between Liverpool Street and East Anglia was introduced; the average acceleration between London and Norwich was twenty-one minutes. Note the continued use of GER pattern white discs instead of lamps to denote the class of train.

CHAPTER 9 - LIVERPOOL STREET

In 1949 suggestions were made that fifteen Bulleid Light Pacifics could be transferred from the Southern Region to the Great Eastern section to improve the line's express passenger services and No. 34059 *Sir Archibald Sinclair* was loaned to Stratford at the end of April. It worked expresses out of Liverpool Street for a few weeks before returning to Nine Elms at the end of May. Nothing further happened until April 1951 when consideration was given to using the Bulleid engines to replace the 'B1' 4-6-0s on the secondary express services to East Anglia and three Light Pacifics, Nos. 34039, 34057 and 34065, were transferred in April/May. No. 34039 *Boscastle*, departing from Liverpool Street with a Holiday Camps express, was allocated to Stratford from May 1951 until March 1952.

F.R. Hebron/Rail Archive Stephenson

This was the reality of the London Terminus up to the early 1960s, smoke and filth, as former streamlined 'B17' 4-6-0 No. 61670 *City of London* departs from Liverpool Street on 7th January 1954. It was built in May 1937 as No. 2870 as *Manchester City* but became *City of London* four months later when streamlined. The streamlining was removed from both 'B17's and they were fitted with 'B1' type 100A boilers at Gorton Works in April 1951 and reclassified as 'B17/6'.

'K3/3' 2-6-0 No. 61880 in the early 1950s about to depart with 'The Scandinavian' which ran to Harwich Parkeston Quay where it connected with the ferries to Denmark. No. 61880 was built at Doncaster in October 1929 as No. 1387, becoming 61880 in June 1949. By 1953 Stratford had sixteen of the class on its books and they were employed mainly on freight work with passenger duties confined to relief and excursion work at busy times.

'Britannia' 4-6-2 No. 70008 *Black Prince* in one of the engine sidings adjacent to the taxi ramp. The Running Foreman's office was situated under the ramp and is just visible immediately to the left of No. 70008. The sidings were quite separate from the turntable and servicing area which was situated in the main throat of the suburban lines on their approaches to the platforms. 70008 has solid axles and plain section coupling rods on the coupled wheels, a modification made to all of the first twenty-five 'Britannia's. These replaced the original hollow axles and fluted coupling rods after a series of incidents in mid-1951 which were traced to the coupled wheels shifting on their axles. No. 70008 was in Crewe Works for this work from 5th December 1951 until 16th February 1952; the loss of the 'Britannia's must have been a bitter blow to the Great Eastern management after the early success of their new engines.

CHAPTER 9 - LIVERPOOL STREET

'B1' 4-6-0 No. 61234 departs from Liverpool Street with 'The Easterling' in 1951. The train name was introduced in June 1950 a year after J.R.R. Tolkien used it in 'Lord of the Rings'. 'The Easterling' was a summer-only service between Liverpool Street and Lowestoft Central and Yarmouth South Town which divided/combined at Beccles. No. 61234 was built by the North British Locomotive Company in September 1947 and was allocated to Stratford until May 1959 when it left for Sheffield Darnall.

F.R. Hebron/Rail Archive Stephenson

'Britannia' 4-6-2 No. 70012 *John of Gaunt* on the turntable as it gets ready to work 'The Broadsman', the 3.30pm departure to Norwich. The name was introduced in June 1950 for the service which conveyed through coaches to Cromer. A longer turntable had to be installed to handle the Pacifics. The large girder bridge in the background carried Primrose Street. The area is unrecognisable today with a massive raft over the tracks supporting huge office blocks.

The "Jazz" service

The running of the "Jazz" services at Liverpool Street was a meticulously organised operation. The cycle, which repeated every ten minutes on each of the four platforms, began with the arrival of the incoming train. Just before the engine came to a stand positioned precisely for the platform water column, the fireman jumped down so that he would be exactly opposite the rear buffers. He then shut off the air hose cocks, disconnected and stowed them. When the fireman gave the signal, the driver reversed the engine to compress the buffers to allow the fireman to uncouple from the train before climbing back onto the platform to put the water bag into the side tank nearest to the column.

Meanwhile, at the other end of the train, the engine which had brought in the previous arrival backed down, coupled up and created the necessary air pressure to enable the brakes to be released. At the same time, the guard would carry out a brake test and transfer the tail lamp to what was now the rear coach.

When the train was ready to depart, the platform staff would advise the signalman by means of an electric plunger. As the train started moving, the water bag was taken from the incoming engine, the tank lid replaced and then the engine would carefully follow out the departing train to the engine bay, with slick work

In July 1920 the GER introduced 'The last word in steam-operated suburban train services', a 50-75% increase in train frequency on the routes to Chingford, Enfield and Palace Gates, produced by a large number of relatively small operating and signal/track improvements. This was done at an estimated cost of £80,000 compared with a price of well over £3 million for electrification. Most noticeable was the handling of trains at Liverpool Street where Platforms 1 to 4 dealt with four trains in each direction every ten minutes during the peak hours. Initially the trains continued to comprise six-a-side four-wheeled stock hauled by 'J69' 0-6-0Ts, but between 1925 and 1927 these were replaced by new 'Quint-Art' sets and the more powerful 'N7' 0-6-2Ts. When the L&NER absorbed the Great Eastern Railway, orders were placed in 1924 to replace the GER coaches which were said to be 'falling apart… …most of the body frames were rotting away'. Twenty-nine 'Quint-Art' sets comprising a Brake Third, Third, Second/Third Composite and a Second and First/Second Composite were followed two years later by four more sets and then another four in 1930. They were designed, unlike the GNR 'Quad-Arts', to be worked as single five-coach trains as well as in ten-coach pairs on the peak-hour services. All were equipped with Westinghouse air brakes which allowed the closely spaced station stops to be tightly timed, enabling the short intervals between trains. Trains would run in at up to 45 mph and stop smoothly at the correct point along the platform thanks to the highly skilled drivers. 'N7/3' 0-6-2T No. 69704, seen waiting to leave Liverpool Street in around 1949, was built as No. 2602 at Doncaster in November 1927 with a L&NER standard round-topped boiler, Westinghouse brake and vacuum ejector, long travel valves and condensing gear which was taken off in 1936. No. 69704 was based at Stratford for almost all of its years in service, except for a few months at Hatfield in late 1952. It had been renumbered as 9704 in 1946 and became BR No. 69704 in March 1949; it was withdrawn in October 1960.

T.G. Hepburn/Rail Archive Stephenson

needed by the signalman to move the points and shunt signal for the bay after the outgoing train had cleared them. In the bay, more water was added to top up the tanks if necessary. The signalman then had to quickly re-set the approach points and signals for the next arrival. He had to change signals about forty times and points around twenty-six times and send forty bell codes every ten minutes, or one action every 7½ seconds, maintaining this for three hours. The change to electrical operation of the points and signals in the late 1930s eased the manual workload but it was still a very demanding job.

The train movements to Platforms 1 to 4 operated in rotation; all trains used one pair of tracks in and out of the station throat, the Up and Down Suburban, which meant that every ten minutes four would arrive and four would depart on them.

Four 'N7' 0-6-2Ts wait for their next workings from Liverpool Street on 13th June 1958.
R.O. Tuck/Rail Archive Stephenson

'N7/3' 0-6-2T No. 69702 departs from Platform 1 on 25th April 1960. It was the first of the L&NER Group Standard 'N7's, built as No. 2600 in November 1927, and was in service allocated to Stratford until March 1961.

CHAPTER 9 - LIVERPOOL STREET

Late 1950s and 1960s

'B12/3' 4-6-0 No. 61535 at Liverpool Street on 24th July 1958. It was built in March 1915 and allocated to Ipswich from May 1948 until the month before its withdrawal in December 1959. Passengers leave the recently arrived 'The East Anglian' in the next platform.

Gresley 'B17' 4-6-0 No. 61665 *Leicester City* stands under the coaling tower at Liverpool Street's engine servicing point adjacent to the turntable as it is oiled ready for its next duty. It was built by R. Stephenson & Co. in January 1937 as L&NER No. 2865, rebuilt as a 'B17/6' with a 'B1' type 100A boiler in August 1949 and was withdrawn in April 1959. This picture was taken while No. 61665 was allocated to Yarmouth South Town shed, from January 1955 until its withdrawal.

Steve Armitage Collection

'J69/1' 0-6-0T No. 68633 at Liverpool Street on 7th August 1959 with a mixed train which includes two single bolster wagons, presumably in use for either moving overhead line gantries or Permanent Way rail removal. It was built by the Great Eastern Railway in September 1904 and was at Stratford from before nationalisation until August 1960, moving to Parkeston Quay for three months until withdrawn. No. 68633 was selected for preservation as part of the National Collection and was restored at Stratford Works to its original condition as GER 'S56' No. 87 before going on display at the Museum of British Transport at Clapham.

A sight for sore eyes with its companion 'J69/1' 0-6-0T No. 68619 on pilot duty, 'N7/4' 0-6-2T No. 69614 with its highly polished lined black livery and fittings offset by red coupling rods. It became Liverpool Street West Side pilot in 1956 and the Stratford enginemen were given an allowance of one hour's overtime to keep the pilot engines immaculate. No. 69614 was withdrawn in December 1960 and replaced by a BTH Type '1' diesel; No. 68619 lasted slightly longer and was in service until October 1961.

CHAPTER 9 - LIVERPOOL STREET

In this picture, taken from the taxi ramp which offered enthusiasts a good view of proceedings, 'Britannia' 4-6-2 No. 70041 *Sir John Moore*, with a badly blowing piston gland, sets off for Norwich on 16th June 1957. No. 70041 was allocated to Stratford from new in March 1953 until February 1958 when the thirteen Stratford 'Britannia's were transferred to Norwich because of a severe shortage of maintenance staff in London. The viaduct carrying the tracks into the adjacent Broad Street terminus is in the background and the cranes are in the Worship Street sidings of Broad Street Goods Depot.

The scene at Liverpool Street on 13th June 1958 with 'B17/6' 4-6-0 No. 61636 *Harlaxton Manor* in the engine dock; 'B1' 4-6-0 No. 61373 and 'Britannia' 4-6-2 No. 70006 *Robert Burns* are waiting to leave with expresses. The bottom of the taxi ramp is on the left. *R.O. Tuck/Rail Archive Stephenson*

Electrification

The L&NER embarked on the electrification at 1,500 volts d.c. overhead of the Liverpool Street-Shenfield suburban route in 1937. Work was suspended during World War Two and did not restart until 1946; the project was finally completed by British Railways in late 1949. Platforms 11 to 18 at Liverpool Street were electrified and colour light signalling was installed at the station and out to Gidea Park. The new service provided up to nineteen trains an hour in each direction in the peak hours compared with four for the steam service it replaced, with a reduction in the journey time for an all-stations train to Shenfield from sixty to forty-five minutes; it produced a forty-six per cent increase in passenger numbers in the first three months of operation and a 40% increase in receipts by March 1950. Ninety-two three-car electric multiple unit sets with open saloons and Third Class only accommodation were built in 1949 and each coach was fitted with air-operated sliding doors to facilitate rapid loading and unloading. A nine-car train had about 500 seats but could carry more than another 500 standing passengers in the peak hours. Four of these sets stand in Platforms 15 to 18 at on 7th June 1956, from left to right: units 25 (for Ilford) 79 and 22 (both Gidea Park) and unidentified (Shenfield). Initially, set numbers were not carried but these were applied in the mid-1950s. All four units have at the front the Driving Brake Motor Second (DBMS) coaches which had a diamond cross-arm pantograph let into a lowered roofline.

The most stylish EMUs built by British Railways were the 'AM9' units for the Clacton and Walton service, the electrification for which had been completed in April 1959. They were based on the Mark 1 main line stock with curved wrap-around driving cabs and finished in lined maroon with yellow connecting doors which rather spoiled their appearance. They were capable of 100mph running and were originally formed as eight two-car and fifteen four-car sets, eight of which included a Griddle Car. The units ran from Liverpool Street as ten-car trains which divided at Thorpe-le-Soken with the front four vehicles going to Walton-on-Naze and the rear six, including the Griddle Car, to Clacton. Two-car set No. 603 was awaiting departure from Liverpool Street on a demonstration run of the new units on 16th February 1963. As Class '309' they worked on the Great Eastern until 1994.

Early 1970s drabness with two types of unit in overall rail blue at Liverpool Street. On the left in Platform 17 is Class '307' No. 110, a BR design four-car outer suburban slam door set built for the Southend service, operating initially on 1,500 d.c. and converted at Eastleigh to 25,000 a.c. in around 1960. On the right in Platform 16 is Class '306' No. 039, a three-car Shenfield 1949 unit. These were also converted to a.c. operation at Stratford Works during which they were extensively rebuilt. The brake compartments and the pantographs were moved from the Driving Motor Brake Second to the intermediate coaches and the roof profiles of the DMBS raised to the full height of the rest of the coach. Stone Faively pantographs replaced the originals and the five-lamp route indicator was replaced by a two-digit roller blind positioned between the windows. The cab fronts were always filthy because the carriage cleaning plants failed to reach these parts.

Diesels

English Electric 2,000 bhp diesel-electric Type '4' D200 departs from Liverpool Street to Norwich on Friday 18th April 1958. This was the official launch of the Great Eastern's new main line diesels with invited guests on board. In September 1958 there were five daily diagrams, one for each of the five then new Type '4' locomotives based at Stratford. They were arranged so that each engine proceeded from one diagram to the next in sequence. They worked between London, Cambridge, Ipswich and Norwich with a daily examination at Liverpool Street, Stratford depot or Norwich; refuelling was usually done at Norwich. These Type '4's hauled eleven-coach trains, compared to the standard nine coaches for the 'Britannia' 4-6-2s which they replaced, and had a scheduled weekly mileage of between 3,600 and 3,900, compared with 2,600 miles for their predecessors.

The first Brush Type '2' diesel-electric, No. D5500, waits to depart with an early afternoon express to Ipswich on 27th May 1958. It arrived at Stratford on 31st October 1957 after completing acceptance trials earlier in the month and was followed onto the Great Eastern lines by over 130 more of the class delivered by mid-1961. Except for three years from June 1959 to June 1962, No. D5500 was always at Stratford. After withdrawal in July 1976 as TOPS No. 31018, it went to the National Railway Museum in January 1977 for preservation and has since operated both on the North Yorkshire Moors Railway and the main line, although it is currently a static exhibit at the National Railway Museum in York.

It looks as if the driver's mate has just left the cab of No. D8400 with his 'Billy can' to fetch a brew as it waits in the engine siding on 20th February 1959. As part of the BR Modernisation Plan Pilot Scheme, ten Type '1' 800bhp Bo-Bo diesel-electrics were built by the North British Locomotive Co. Ltd in 1958 and allocated to Stratford. They were based closely on the LM&SR prototype No. 10800 and proved equally unsuccessful. No. D8400 failed several times during its acceptance trials at Doncaster Works and this was a portent of things to come with the other nine locomotives having similar problems. All ten were finally put out of their misery in 1968, unlike their Type '2' compatriots without any thought of re-engining.

There are four different classes of diesel in this early 1961 view from the platform end. In the centre, English Electric Type '4' No. D205 is arriving while an unidentified English Electric Type '3' waits in one of the engine sidings. On the left a Brush Type '2' is waiting to depart and on the extreme right a BTH Type '1' on station pilot duty can just be glimpsed.

Above: Steam had been banished from Liverpool Street since the end of 1962 and the station was noticeably much cleaner on 1st October 1964. There is much parcels activity in evidence as English Electric 1,750 bhp Type '3' No. D6701 waits to leave from Platform 9. The class was the first of the second generation of main line diesels delivered to the Great Eastern from the end of 1960 and they took over most of the express duties which had up until then been handled by the lower-powered Brush Type '2's. No. D6701 was at Stratford until July 1967 when it went north to Wath. As TOPS No. 37707 it returned to Stratford between 1982 and 1986 and again in 1988; it continued to move around the country until its eventual withdrawal in 2011.

Green liveried Class '47' No. 1777 with an unidentified Class '31' behind on 22nd March 1973. Like many of the Stratford locomotives, its BR emblem has been worn away by frequent trips through the carriage cleaning plants. The 2,750 bhp Brush diesels had displaced the 1,750 bhp English Electric Class '37's from the principal Great Eastern line expresses in April 1966 when thirteen of the class, including No. 1777, were transferred to Stratford. As with many of the Class '47's, it was renumbered several times under TOPS, becoming 47182 in March 1974, 47598 in 1983 and finally 47742 in 1995.

10 – Liverpool Street Approaches

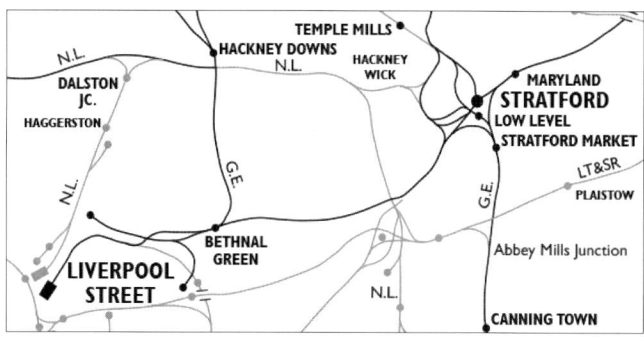

There were six tracks from the throat of Liverpool Street as far as Bethnal Green, four for the main line to Stratford and two for Hackney, which immediately doubled to four tracks as far as Hackney Downs.

The first of the post-First World War 'N7' 0-6-2Ts No. 69602 approaches Bethnal Green from Hackney Downs in May 1959. Note the four tracks merging into two and the switched diamond.

Bethnal Green

'B17/6' 4-6-0 No. 61656 *Leeds United* with a Down express runs through Bethnal Green on 28th February 1959. Twenty-five of the class were named after football clubs in the L&NER area and the remainder similarly commemorated country houses, the first of which, *Sandringham*, gave its name to the class.

'B17' 4-6-0 No. 61657 *Doncaster Rovers* reaches the top of the 1 in 70 climb from Liverpool Street and approaches the Bethnal Green platforms with a Down express on 30th August 1958. It had been rebuilt to a 'B17/6' with a 'B1' type Diagram 100A boiler in October 1950 and was transferred to March from Cambridge in March 1956; it was withdrawn there in June 1960. There was some interesting pointwork at the Liverpool Street end of the station which allowed trains to cross all the way over the six tracks in both directions.

CHAPTER 10 - LIVERPOOL STREET APPROACHES

The pioneer Great Eastern Railway 'N7' 0-6-2T No. 69600, arrives at Bethnal Green with the 9.19am Liverpool Street to Chingford on 11th October 1958. It was built in January 1915, one of a pair of 0-6-2Ts designed by A.J. Hill to replace the 2-4-2Ts which had hitherto been employed on the London suburban services. For comparison, No. 1000 had saturated steam and the other, No. 1001, was superheated. The First World War halted further production and no more of the class were built until 1921. No. 1000 was renumbered as 8000 in 1924 and was superheated in 1929; it was rebuilt as an 'N7/4' with a round-topped firebox in 1943 and was withdrawn in February 1959. Note the stylish L&NER electric lighting globes which replaced the GER gas lamps.

'N7/3' 0-6-2T No. 69729 with an Up Empty Coaching Stock train of main line stock on 10th June 1959. It was one of the last five of the class built at Doncaster in 1928 – the final version of the 'N7' class with round-topped firebox and long-travel valve gear.

'K3/2' 2-6-0 No. 61951 approaches the station with a Down Parcels on 14th April 1960. It was a former 30A engine which went to Parkeston in March 1958. No. 61951 was built by the North British Locomotive Company as L&NER No. 2450 in October 1935 and was withdrawn from Doncaster in November 1962.

'N7/5' 0-6-2T No. 69658 with a Down train arriving at Bethnal Green on 18th October 1960, a month before the end of the "Jazz" service. It was built by Robert Stephenson & Co. in 1925, originally with condensing gear which was removed in 1936, and rebuilt with a round-topped boiler in August 1950; it was withdrawn in April 1961. New fluorescent tube station signs have now replaced the totems and the overhead wires for the electrification have been installed.

'N7/5' 0-6-2T No. 69671 ready to depart from Bethnal Green for Liverpool Street on 22nd March 1960. It was the last of the class built for the L&NER by R. Stephenson & Co., entering service in January 1926. They differed from the final Great Eastern Railway engines, having reduced height boiler mountings and condensers to allow them to work within the restricted gauge of the Metropolitan Widened Lines. No. 69671 was rebuilt in January 1950 as an 'N7/5' with round-topped firebox but retained its original short-travel valves.

'Britannia' 4-6-2 No. 70008 *Black Prince* approaches Bethnal Green with an Up express on 1st October 1960. It was allocated to Norwich from new in April 1951 until September 1961, moving to March before spending its final three years at Carlisle Kingmoor.

Two diesel-hauled expresses racing up from Liverpool Street approaching Bethnal Green station on 30th August 1958. Both locomotives are Brush 1,250 hp Type '2' A1A-A1A diesel-electrics. On the left, No. D5500 is heading the 11.12a.m. to Gorleston Holiday Camp; on the right (on the Down Slow line) is No. D5506 with the 11.8a.m. to Walton-on-Naze. No. D5500 went to the National Railway Museum for preservation in 1977 but No. D5506 was not so fortunate and was scrapped after withdrawal in January 1980.
B.W. Brooksbank

Three Class '306' units led by newly repainted set No. 010 on an Up service to Liverpool Street at Bethnal Green in the early 1970s. All of the '306' fleet were withdrawn in 1980/81.

Hackney Downs

Hackney Downs station opened in 1872 and by 1873 had access to Enfield Town, Walthamstow, Chingford and the Cambridge line. 'N7/3' 0-6-2T No. 69720 arrives there with an Up train in the late 1950s. At first glance it appears that the line the train is running on is signalled for bi-directional running. However, the signal on the right is a repeater with the same number as the one on the left.

Brush Type '2' No. D5512 with the 10.27am Hunstanton-Liverpool Street at Hackney Downs on 21st March 1959. The first twenty locomotives in the class, later Class '31/1', were nicknamed 'Toffee Apples' by drivers because of the shape of the control key needed when changing driving ends. No. D5512 was allocated to Stratford from new in June 1958 until withdrawal in November 1976. The first coach in the train is crossing the bridge over the former North London Railway line between Dalston Junction and Poplar.　　　　　　　　　　　　　　　　　　　　　　　　　　　　*K.L. Cook/Rail Archive Stephenson*

'B1' 4-6-0 No. 61104 on the 12.12pm Brandon-Liverpool Street passes through Hackney Downs on 21st March 1959. Formerly a Stratford engine, it was allocated to Cambridge the previous month although its stay there was brief, moving to Sheffield Darnall in May. *K.L. Cook/Rail Archive Stephenson*

'L1' 2-6-4T No. 67725 bunker-first with the 2.48pm Liverpool Street-Broxbourne at Hackney Downs on 21st March 1959. It was built by BR at Darlington Works in June 1948 and was in service until the end of 1960. At this date Stratford had over twenty of the class on its books.
K.L. Cook/Rail Archive Stephenson

CHAPTER 10 - LIVERPOOL STREET APPROACHES

One of the two beautifully cleaned Liverpool Street station pilots, GER 'J69/1' 0-6-0T No. 68619, has been called to take the place of a failed 'N7' on the 5.27pm Liverpool Street to Chingford train near Hackney Downs on 7th May 1959. The J69's had been the mainstay of the London services until they were displaced by the 'N7's from 1925 onwards which were able to handle the ten-coach 'Quint-Art' sets that were almost fifty tons heavier than the GER rakes of sixteen four-wheelers. No. 68619 was a Liverpool Street station pilot from January 1948, initially painted in L&NER lined green which it kept until June 1953 when it was repainted in plain black. Lining was later added and in September 1959 it was given GER blue livery with red lining and coupling rods and the GER crest below the number on the bunker side. Despite its final years spent in the limelight, it was not preserved and instead No. 68633 was chosen for the National Collection. *K.L. Cook/Rail Archive Stephenson*

Stratford station

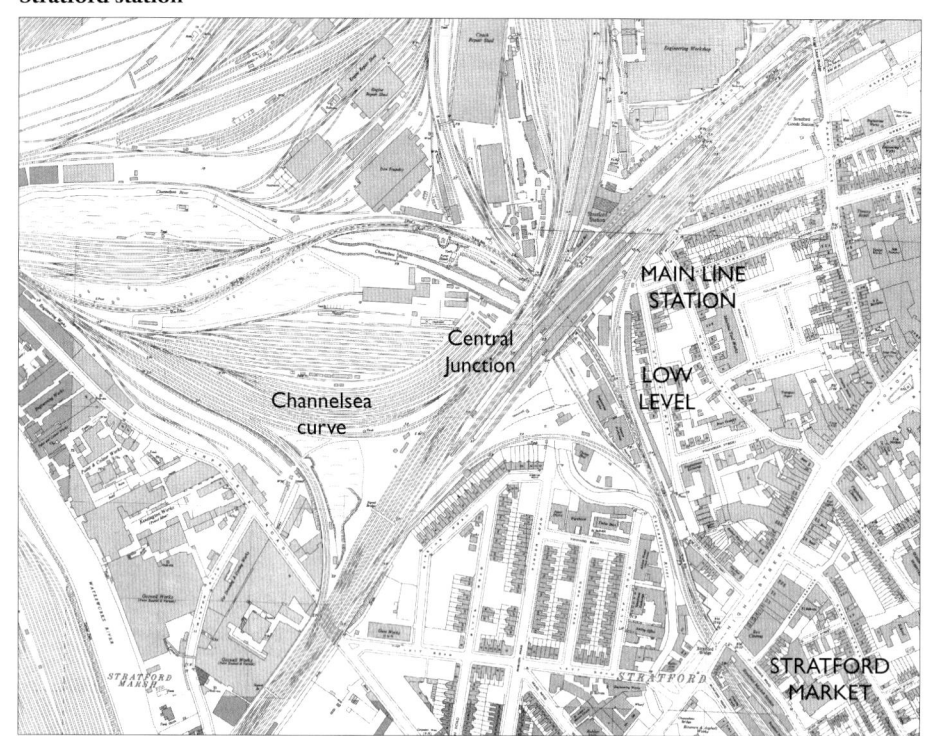

Stratford station was in the middle of complex set of junctions and loops formed by the intersection of the main London to Colchester and Norwich line, the Lea Valley line to Cambridge, the North Woolwich line via Stratford Market to the Low Level station, and the Channelsea curve to the North London line.

A 'J15' 0-6-0 takes a Permanent Way crane and its six-wheel match truck towards the station in 1948; the Loughton platforms are on the right.

'L1' 2-6-4T No. 67702 in apple green livery passes through Stratford on a Class 'F' freight in September 1948. It still has LNER lettering on the tank sides but has received its BR number. No. 67702 had entered service from Darlington Works in January 1948 as No. 9001 but was quickly renumbered in May when it was decided that the class should take the number series beginning with 67701. In the background is the recently completed Stratford Station signal box which was part of the modernisation scheme which had started before the Second World War.

CHAPTER 10 - LIVERPOOL STREET APPROACHES

'B12' 4-6-0 No. 61575 at Stratford on an Up train in 1948. This was one of the ten engines built for the L&NER in late 1928 by Beyer, Peacock & Co., originally with Lentz poppet valve gear but this was removed in 1932. As with all except one of the English-based engines in the class, it was rebuilt to a 'B12/3' with a larger boiler and a re-designed front end, in July 1933, and became No. 61575 in April 1948.

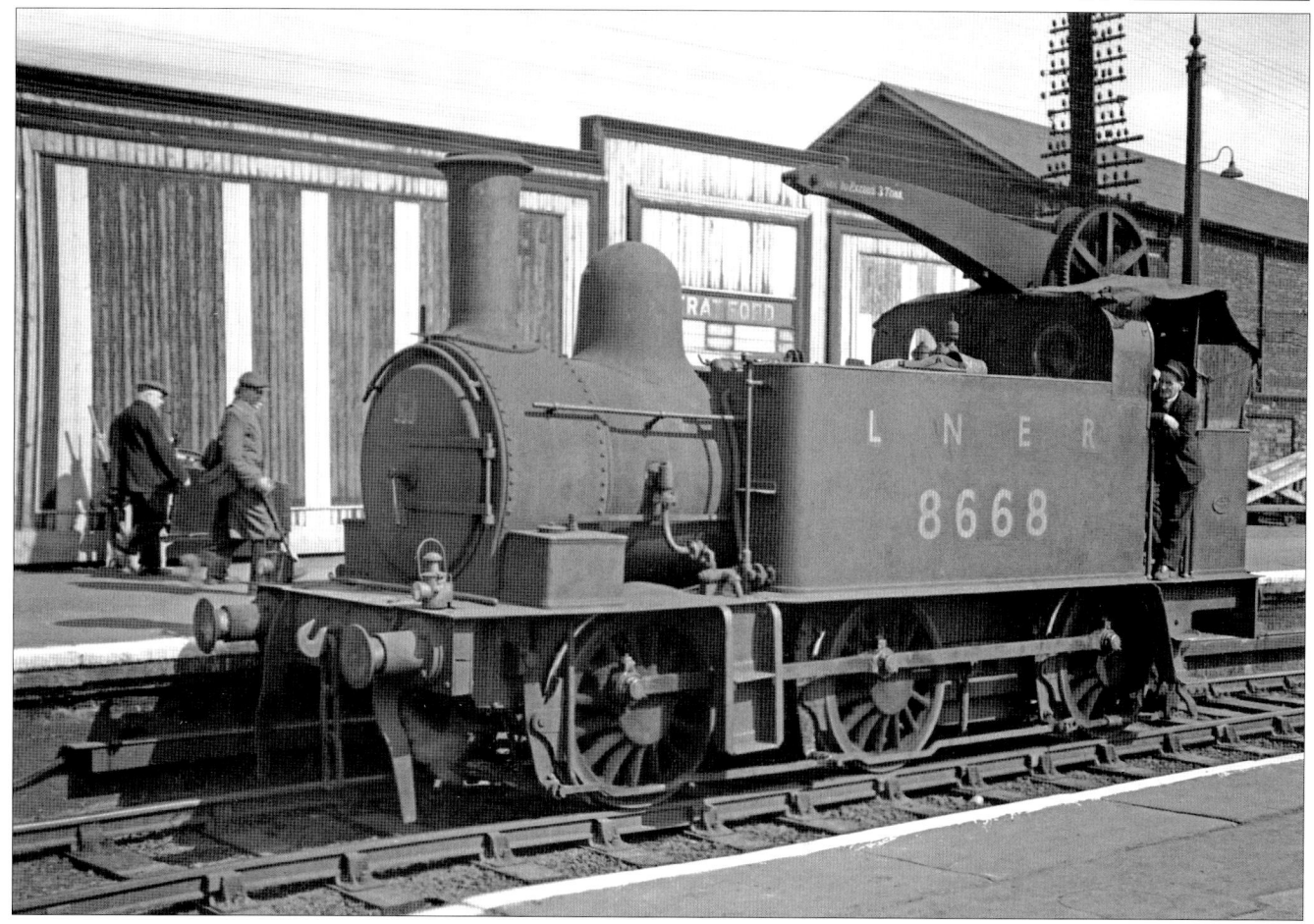

L&NER 'J92' 0-6-0 crane tank No. 8668 in the Loughton platform in 1948 in a very rare view of one of these engines outside the works. This was one of five 0-6-0Ts built as GER Class '204' to the design of S.W. Johnson, three of which were rebuilt between 1881 and 1883 with a 3-ton capacity crane at the rear end for use in Stratford Works, and were given the letters B, C and D in place of their numbers. They were used to move dead engines around the works and to take wagon loads of boilers, wheels, etc. to and from the Old Works adjacent to Stratford passenger station. The crane, which has no hook or chain, had been taken out of use by the 1920s and its supporting iron framework replaced by a wooden boarded arrangement to give the enginemen more protection. No E8668, formerly 'C', received its number in June 1946 and was renumbered as 68668 in February 1950 but was withdrawn in November 1952 after becoming 'Departmental No. 35' in September of that year.

Stratford shed 'B12/3' 4-6-0 No. 61573 passes through the station with an Up train for Liverpool Street on 26th March 1949. This was one of the ten engines built for the L&NER in 1928 by Beyer, Peacock & Co., originally with Lentz poppet valve gear, but this was removed in December 1931. As with all except one of the English-based engines in the class, it was rebuilt to a 'B12/3' with a larger boiler and a re-designed front end, in July 1933.

T.G. Hepburn/Rail Archive Stephenson

'B1' 4-6-0 No. E1051 passes Stratford with the Up 'East Anglian' on 26th March 1949. It had been built by the North British Locomotive Co. in June 1946, going to Norwich shed from new, and became No. 61051 in March 1950. The masts are in place for the Shenfield electrification.

T.G. Hepburn/Rail Archive Stephenson

CHAPTER 10 - LIVERPOOL STREET APPROACHES

GER 'J17' 0-6-0 No. 65543 passes Stratford with an Up grain train in July 1951. It seems that there was a shortage of purpose-built grain wagons and some L&NER coal hoppers have been modified with an additional top bar allowing a wagon sheet to be used to keep the load dry. The overhead wires are now fully operational. No. 65543 was rebuilt from a 'J16' to a 'J17' in March 1921 when it was fitted with a Belpaire boiler; it was withdrawn in May 1955.
C.R.L. Coles/Rail Archive Stephenson

Stratford allocated 'J50/3' 0-6-0T No. 68963 passes through the station with an Up Class 'K' goods in July 1951. This was one of the class built by the L&NER between 1926 and 1939 following its adoption as a Group Standard design. No. 68963 entered service in December as 1926 as L&NER No. 1063 and was withdrawn in February 1962. Note the first and second wagons still reveal their pre-nationalisation origins. *C.R.L. Coles/Rail Archive Stephenson*

'N7/3' 0-6-2T No. 69721 passing the Engineering Workshop and Test House as it runs towards the Cambridge line platforms. On the right, Ivatt Class '4' 2-6-0 No. 43108 from South Lynn on the M&GN line, which appears to be jacked-up, was in the Works for a General overhaul from 21st April to 20th June 1958. The GER water column on the left has a cast iron plate marked 'NO WATER AT' – the space below was used to hold a painted steel plate telling the crews where they would be unable to top up their tanks.

A brand new Wickham two-car DMU, with Driving Trailer Composite No. E56173 leading, in the Enfield platforms in 1958; it had been delivered to Stratford in April 1958. Two sets regularly worked the Upminster-Romford branch but this one was transferred to Cambridge six months later. Only five sets were built to this design and they employed an unusual form of body construction with a frame made of square section steel tube which enabled the conventional heavy steel underframe to be dispensed with. They became Class '109' under TOPS.

CHAPTER 10 - LIVERPOOL STREET APPROACHES

English Electric Type '4' No. D201 roars through Stratford with an Up express in 1961. Although initially allocated to Stratford in April 1958 it moved to the Great Northern main line the following month and did not return to Stratford until June 1961. It stayed on the Great Eastern until January 1967 when it moved to the London Midland Region. Renumbered to 40001 in 1974, it was withdrawn from Carlisle in 1984.

Brush Type '2' No. D5586 brings an Up express through Stratford while 'AM8' EMU No. 148 picks up passengers in the platform, probably on the same day in 1961 as the previous picture. D5586 was originally allocated to Hornsey and then to Finsbury Park before it was transferred to March, Cambridgeshire in January 1961 and to Stratford in June. It moved around the country extensively during its thirty-year working life with spells at Bristol, Immingham, Tinsley, Leeds and York.

The last of the ten North British Type '1' 800 bhp Bo-Bos, No. D8409 with a long goods train comes round the Channelsea curve off the North London line in 1959. The overhead wires are not yet fully in place.

No English Electric Type '1 Bo-Bos were allocated to Stratford until Devons Road shed closed in 1964 when Nos D8013-8019 were transferred there. No. D8014 brings what appears to be an excursion from the London Midland Region round the curve from Channelsea Junction and the North London line towards the station on 7th June 1959. In their early years the class rarely worked in the pairs as they commonly did from the late 1960s onwards. No. D8014 moved to Immingham together with No. D8015 in October 1965 in exchange for Nos D8054 and D8055, and became No. 20014 in January 1973 but only lasted for three years before it was withdrawn by the LMR Nottingham Division.

CHAPTER 10 - LIVERPOOL STREET APPROACHES

'AM6' EMU No. 43 stands in Platform 7 at Stratford on a Shenfield service in the mid-1950s.

'AM6' EMU No. 65 runs through Stratford on a Southend Victoria service in 1959. Electrification had been extended from Shenfield to Southend at the end of 1956. The train consists of three of the 1949-built d.c. three-car units with the cross-arm pantograph DBMS leading. The fleet of ninety-two sets was built by Metropolitan Cammell and the Birmingham Railway Carriage & Wagon and was converted to a.c. operation in 1960/61.

'AM2' EMU set No. 221 is at the front of an eight-car working to Southend Victoria service on 6th November 1960. The four-car 'AM2' units to a BR standard slam-door design were built between 1958 and 1960 for the London Tilbury & Southend electrification but were deployed on other services until the Tilbury electrification was completed at the end of 1961. Some were used in the interim on routes newly converted from d.c. to a.c. operation, the work on which was completed during the weekend of 4th – 6th November 1960, so this picture is probably one of the first a.c. services.

K.L. Cook/Rail Archive Stephenson

CHAPTER 10 - LIVERPOOL STREET APPROACHES 145

Now in dull overall blue with full yellow ends, Class '302' EMU No. 217 with an Up service at Stratford in the early 1970s paired with what looks like a Class '308' at the rear. Note the 1F73 headcode.

The permanent way workers pause for Class '308/3' EMU No. 453 running as Empty Coaching Stock to pass through on its way to Ilford depot in the early 1970s. This was one of three three-car sets additional to the main 'AM8' four-car fleet built in 1961.

11 – Stratford Shed, Works and Temple Mills yard

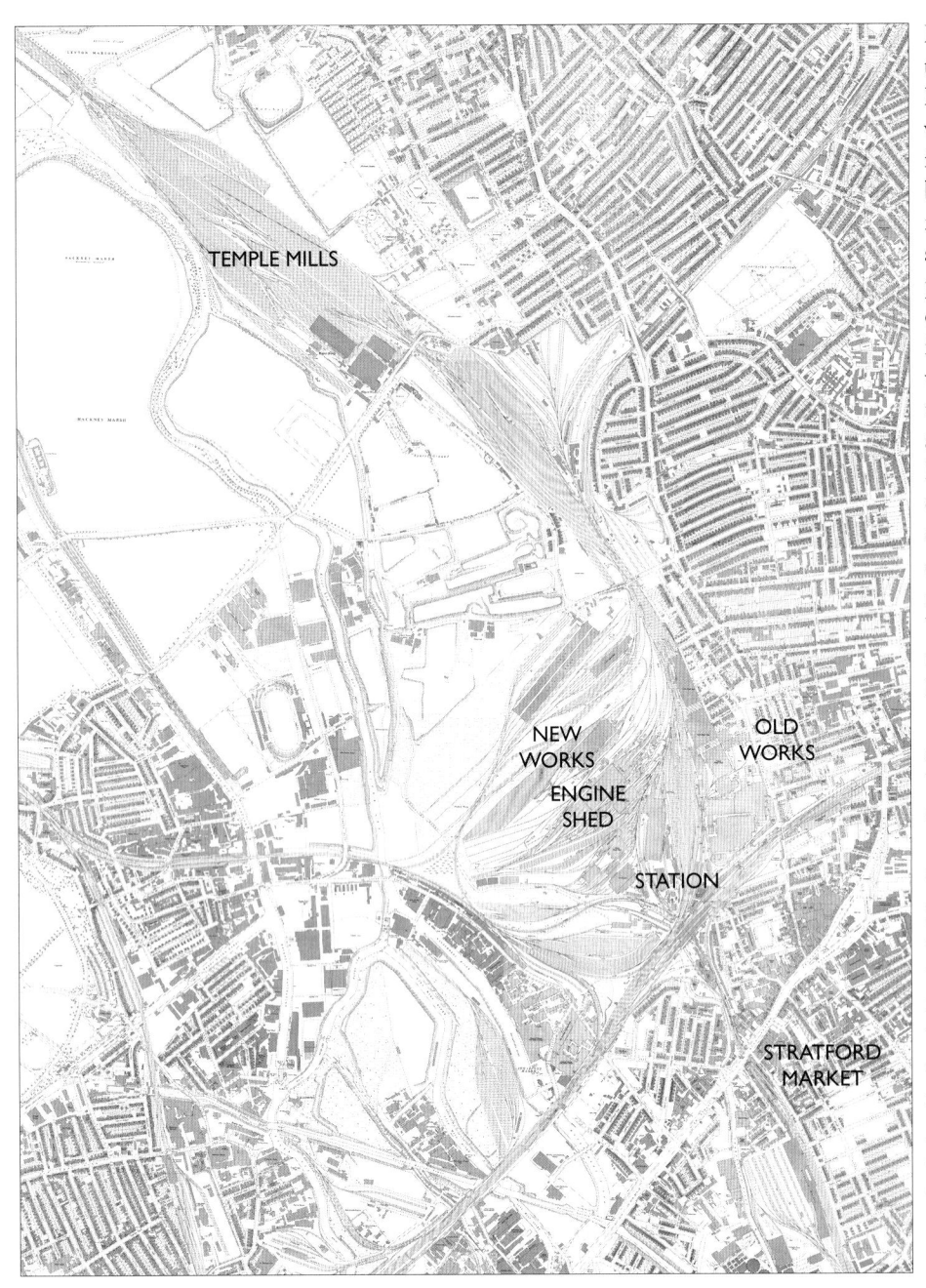

In 1847 the Eastern Counties Railway transferred their locomotive works from Romford to Stratford where a New Town was built to house the workforce. The fifteen acre site occupied a triangular area between the Colchester and Cambridge main lines. Together with the running shed and carriage sheds, it was extended piecemeal over the next three decades to cover more than 100 acres in total, with facilities for locomotive, carriage and wagon building and repairs in addition to what had become the largest running shed on the Great Eastern Railway. Expansion continued during the early 20th century, and all in the middle of what had developed into a complex set of junctions and loops formed by the intersection of the main London to Norwich line, the North Woolwich line from the Low Level station, the Lea Valley line to Cambridge and the link to the North London line. By the 1923 Grouping the site had over twenty separate shops or sheds even though Wagon construction and repair had been moved away to Temple Mills in 1896.

Stratford shed and Works was huge. On a Sunday in its British Railways' peak during the 1950s, it would regularly contain over 230 engines and another thirty-five or more in the works (it was not always easy to 'bunk' the various works buildings). A visit took a whole afternoon but it was one never to be forgotten to a traveller from distant parts! Even for the locals there were always visitors that had worked freights down from Whitemoor yard, or 'foreign' engines in for works attention. You always bumped into other enthusiasts on your pilgrimage and only occasionally were thrown out – it was worth the effort!

The Shed

The shed which was coded 30A by British Railways had between 350 and 400 engines allocated there during the 1950s, covering express passenger, suburban passenger, all types of freight and shunting duties.

There were two running sheds, both of the 'straight through' patten. The larger was the twelve-road 'Jubilee Shed' built in 1887 and the smaller, 1871 'New Shed' which had six roads, three of which were used for repair work. The layout had been remodelled in the 1930s when a new 70ft electrically operated turntable was installed in addition to the existing 65ft table. A large new mechanical coaling plant replaced the hand coaling stage which had required thirty-six men to operate it. The long reinforced concrete bunker had a capacity of 800 tons or about 1½ days' normal consumption and was fed from wagons moved by an electric capstan and discharged onto a system of conveyor belts. The bunker fed eight chutes, each of which could coal an engine in a few seconds. The shed closed to steam in October 1962.

Steam days

'D15' 4-4-0 No. 62502 at Stratford shed on 3rd February 1952 was withdrawn officially on the following day. It was built at Stratford in 1900, superheated in 1916 and rebuilt as a 'D15/2' with a larger boiler and Belpaire firebox in 1936; the BR number was applied in March 1950.

This is what was underneath the bodywork on a tram engine, as illustrated by unfrocked 'J70' 0-6-0T No. 68219 on 11th October 1953. It had been withdrawn two months earlier after over forty years in service.

Gresley 'B17/6' 4-6-0 No. 61651 *Derby County* alongside 'B1' No. 61149 outside the twelve-road main running shed, known as the 'Jubilee Shed', in 1953. No. 61651 was allocated to Stratford from October 1951 when it arrived from Colwick until December 1953 when it left for Colchester. It was rebuilt to a 'B17/6' with a 100A 'B1' type boiler in June 1953.

One of 30A's 'J17' 0-6-0s No. 65563 in October 1956 flanked by two Ivatt 2-6-0s, Class '2' No. 46468 on the left and a Class '4' on the right. No. 46468 from Colchester was at Stratford for a Light Casual repair, the only occasion when it was not overhauled at Darlington, where it had been built in 1951. This is one of the repair sheds, known as the 'New Shed', and was much lighter and airy than the running shed. In diesel days it was used to service DMUs and to store the 204bhp shunters.

CHAPTER 11 - STRATFORD SHED, WORKS AND TEMPLE MILLS YARD

'D16/3' 4-4-0 No. 62618 ex-works in immaculate condition in around 1957. The two turntables seem to have been an under-photographed part of the Stratford complex; this is the one at the northern end. No. 62618 had been allocated to Cambridge since before nationalisation but moved to King's Lynn in March 1958. It was one of ten engines built by the L&NER as a 'D15' in 1923 and became a 'D16/3' when rebuilt in January 1929 with a round-topped firebox. It was withdrawn in November 1959.

Freight engines are everywhere at Stratford on a Saturday in 1958. Those which can be identified are 'J39' Nos. 64784 and 64873 and 'J15' 0-6-0 No. 65449; all three were allocated to 30A at this date. The 'New Works' building is in the centre background and a corner of the 'Jubilee Shed' is on the right of the picture.

Stratford 'L1' 2-6-4T No. 67716 in front of the massive coaling plant with 'N7/3' No. 69710 on the left and 'J68' 0-6-0T No. 68642 on the right, probably in 1961. The plant was very close to the running shed and in constant use so did not help the atmosphere in the area.

'N7/5' 0-6-2T No. 69646 and an unidentified 'B1' 4-6-0 around the same date as the above picture. No. 69646 was built at Gorton in October 1926 and rebuilt with a round-topped firebox in May 1954; it was withdrawn in September 1962. The shed in the background is the remains of the twelve-road main running 'Jubilee Shed', which was built in 1887 and heavily rebuilt by British Railways after the Second World War. Half of it was demolished in the late 1950s to make way for the diesel shed which can just be glimpsed on the left. The coaling stage was reduced to rubble by September 1962.

Diesel shunters

In the late 1950s and early 1960s Stratford was home to an eclectic mix of mainly low-powered diesel shunters. It also had a fleet of larger 350 bhp machines based on the LM&SR twin-motor design. During the 1960s Stratford had to supply over forty diesel shunters for the surrounding goods yards, mostly the larger 350 bhp type, but a number of the smaller 180 bhp and 204 bhp shunters with their lower axle loading and shorter wheelbase to negotiate sharp curves were needed at Poplar, Mile End, Blackwall and Bow Creek.

Barclay 153 bhp 0-4-0 diesel shunter with mechanical transmission, No. 11503 at Stratford on 28th September 1956. It had entered service at the start of the year and became No. D2953 in October 1960. After withdrawal in June 1966 No. D2953 was sold to Thames Matex Ltd for use at their oil refinery in Essex. It was subsequently purchased for preservation and is based at the Heritage Shunters Trust site in Rowsley.

Ruston & Hornsby 165 bhp diesel-mechanical shunter No. D2957 on 24th May 1959 alongside the Diesel Repair Shop, formerly the GER High Meads Locomotive Repair Shop until it was converted for diesel use in 1958. One of two of the type bought by BR in 1956, it was originally No 11507 until April 1958 and was allocated to Stratford from February 1957 until August 1966 when it was transferred to Goole, but immediately went into store before withdrawal in March 1967.

English Electric 500 bhp prototype diesel-electric shunter No. D226 at Stratford on 24th May 1958 had arrived at Stratford on loan in 1957. It was transferred to the Western Region in October 1959 from where it was withdrawn at the end of 1960 and returned to English Electric where it was used as a works shunter until 1966 when it was placed on permanent loan to the Keighley & Worth Valley Railway. Even the spotters wore suits in those days!

The 500 bhp diesel-hydraulic twin of No. D226 with Krupp-Lysholm transmission, No. D227 at Stratford on 30th May 1959. As with No. D226, it was on loan to Stratford and was noted on Empty Coaching Stock duties at Liverpool Street as well as on transfer freight work, but was withdrawn in September 1959 and returned to English Electric for disposal. Both locomotives were painted black with a garish orange stripe down the side ending in 'whiskers' over the bonnet. They were renumbered in August 1959 as D0226 and D0227, to avoid clashing with two new English Electric Type '4's entering service.

CHAPTER 11 - STRATFORD SHED, WORKS AND TEMPLE MILLS YARD

No. D2999 at Stratford on 26th March 1961 was one of five 180 bhp diesel-electric 0-4-0s built by Brush Traction in co-operation with Beyer, Peacock & Co. in 1958. It was loaned to BR in January 1960 and used in the Mile End goods yard. It was purchased by British Railways in September 1960 and given the stock number D2999 and had just been repainted into green livery when photographed. It was based at Stratford until withdrawn in October 1967. Barclay 153 bhp 0-4-0 No. D2954, which became TOPS No 01001 in 1973 and ended its days working on the breakwater at Holyhead, is next to it.

Diesel shunters Nos 12108 and 12130 in the Stratford TMD on 27th June 1964. The immediate predecessors of the ubiquitous '08' BR standard shunters, these were two of the LM&SR designed twin-motor 0-6-0 diesel shunters powered by English Electric 350 bhp 6KT engines and were built at Darlington in 1952. Stratford had an allocation of at least a dozen of the class until the end of the 1960s; both No. 12103 and No. 12130 were withdrawn from there in December 1971 and June 1972 respectively.

Dieselisation

Main line dieselisation began on the Great Eastern in 1958 with the first Brush Type '2' and English Electric Type '4' designs and, as with the diesel shunters, a number of other classes soon followed, most notably the ill-fated NBL Type '1' Bo-Bos and their more successful BTH equivalents. When these classes were withdrawn, they were replaced for a short time by English Electric Type '1's until work for them disappeared. The Type '2' power classification saw another poor North British design, which were all transferred to Scotland by mid-1960, and a small number of the BR Sulzer, later Class '24', which were there for a couple of years until they were concentrated on the London Midland Region leaving only the much more numerous Brush design in this power category. English Electric Type '3's took over express duties from steam in 1961, and were supplemented by five more Type '4's.

Half of the 'Jubilee Shed' was demolished in 1957 and a 300ft long, four-road diesel maintenance shed was built on the site in 1958. It had bays at each end giving a capacity of sixteen locomotives at any one time. Raised platforms 4ft 6in. above rail level and lowered floors or pits were provided to allow work to be carried out on two levels. The shed was used for running repair work and scheduled maintenance only; removal of an engine or generator was done in works. Servicing of DMUs and shunters was carried out in a new three-road shed. The depot remained in use until July 2001.

	December 1959	February 1965
Shunters	54	54
NBL Type '1'	10	10
BTH Type '1'	2	21
EE Type '1'		7
Brush Type '2'	13	42
NBL Type '2'	10	
BR Sulzer Type '2'	2	
EE Type '3'		30
EE Type '4'	5	10
	96	174
DMU power cars	47	
Booked diagrams		
Shunters		40
Main-line		94

A posed picture in one of the new diesel sheds taken on 7th January 1958 with Brush Type '2' No. D5501 and a Derby 'Lightweight' DMU, with an English Electric Type '1' and a diesel shunter in the background. By the 1970s this building was used primarily for servicing DMUs, although initially they were maintained in the 'New Shed'.

CHAPTER 11 - STRATFORD SHED, WORKS AND TEMPLE MILLS YARD

Two pairs of different Type '2' diesel-electric designs share the depot and yard in late 1960 or early 1961. The two in front of the main Traction Maintenance Depot building ('C' Shed) are No. D5636 which was built by Brush in July 1960 and Sulzer No. D5050 from Crewe Works in November 1959. No. D5636 was allocated to Stratford until it moved to March in June 1962 and No. D5050 was there from September 1960 until March 1961 when it was transferred to Finsbury Park. The Brush survived much longer than the Sulzer, eventually taken out of service as TOPS No. 31212 in December 1991 whereas the latter only lasted as TOPS 24050 until August 1975.

North British Type '1' 800 bhp Bo-Bo No. D8401 in 'B' shed with its raised servicing platforms which was built on the site of the steam running shed and was a standard Eastern Region design similar to those at Tinsley and Finsbury Park. There is an unidentified BR Sulzer Type '2' behind.

The ten Type '1' 800bhp Bo-Bo diesel-electrics built by the North British Locomotive Co. Ltd. in 1958 were all allocated to Stratford during their short and unsuccessful working lives. Inevitably they were selected for early withdrawal under British Rail's National Traction Plan of 1965 and they were all taken out of service during 1968 without acquiring their TOPS Class '16' numbers. No. D8403 was parked next to BR Sulzer Type '2' No. D5035 which was at Stratford from new in February 1960 until March 1961, suggesting that this picture was taken in early 1960.

Works

1. Loco. machine shop
2. Loco. machine shop extension
3. Erecting shop
4. Loco. smithy
5. Boiler shop
6. Boiler mounting shop
7. Loco. wheel shop
8. Wheel fitting shop
9. Carriage paint shop
10. Carriage saw mills etc.
11. Body shop
12. Carriage repair & lifting shop
13. Road van shop
14. Carriage dept. smithy
15. Carriage shed
16. Carriage dept. extension shop
17. Carriage wheel & stamping shop
18. Iron foundry
19. Loco. paint shop
20. Boiler repair & tube shop
21. Tender shop
22. Running shed
23. Running shed
24. New engine repair shop
25. New carriage paint shop
26. Oil fuel store
27. Timber stores
28. Power station
29. Gas works

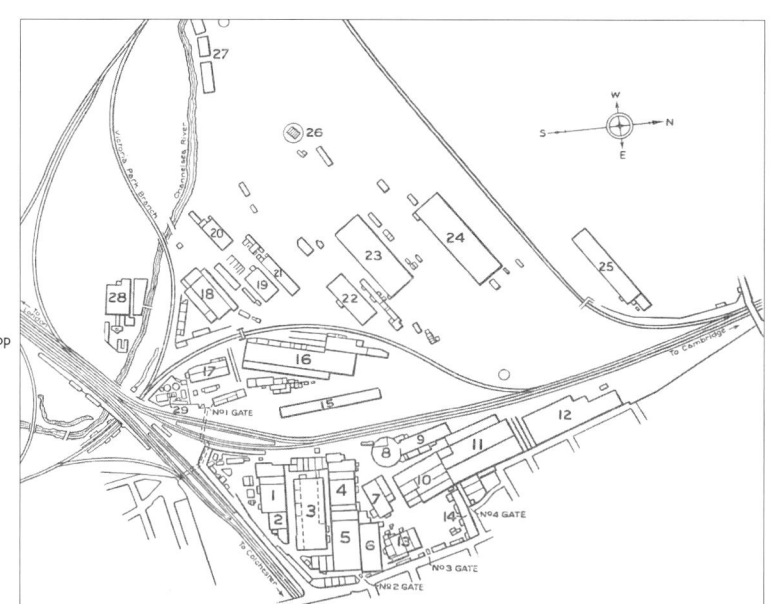

The 1921 plan above that only shows the running lines includes: 22 – 'New Shed'; 23 – 'Jubilee Shed'; 24 – High Meads Engine Repair Shop (New Works)

The locomotive works inherited by the L&NER in 1923 comprised twelve separate shops covering machining, boiler, wheel, tender, erecting, and painting, most of which were grouped on the original site between the Colchester and Cambridge lines. However, the main Works building in the 20th century was the High Meads Engine Repair Shop on the other side of the Cambridge line which had been opened under the Locomotive Superintendent A.J. Hill during the First World War to increase the Works' capacity. It was 480ft long with three bays and could accommodate forty to fifty steam locomotives. It was refurbished in 1958 to deal with repairs to the incoming diesel fleet, albeit with a reduced capacity of eighteen locomotives.

A man on his cycle is probably about to overtake Drewry 204 bhp diesel-mechanical 0-6-0 shunter No. 11112 as it runs through the Works in the late 1950s. It went to Ipswich when new in September 1954 and moved to Stratford in August 1955, was renumbered as D2211 in July 1959 and withdrawn in 1970. In the left background is Works Boiler Trolley No. 5 which had been converted from an ancient GER locomotive.

'Y4' 0-4-0T No. 68126 was the second of the five engines in the class, built in October 1914 as GER No. 228; it became No. 68126 in June 1949 and was withdrawn in October 1957. It was built for working at Mile End goods yard for which it had a reduced height compared to the standard loading gauge. After nationalisation, coal rails were fitted to the coal box on the top of the rear tank, but coal has still spilled over onto the firebox and tank top.

'N7/5' 0-6-2T No. 69668 in Stratford 'New Works' erecting shop on 15th January 1961. This building was the High Meads Engine Repair Shop which had been opened during the First World War to increase the Works' capacity, hence the name 'New Works'.

Stratford 'J15' 0-6-0 No. 65464, also on 15th January 1961, was repaired and worked for another eighteen months before withdrawal. The 'J15' was introduced in 1883, designed by T.W. Worsdell and was the most numerous GER class, eventually totalling 289 engines as more were built under J. Holden and A.J. Hill after Worsdell retired. No. 65464, built in 1912, was one of the final batch of twenty engines.

In the 'Old Works' adjacent to the Cambridge line platforms, Departmental No. 33, a 'Y4' 0-4-0T which was No. 68129 until transferred to Departmental Stock in September 1952. For its wheel arrangement, the 'Y4' was exceptionally large and powerful. They did not have a rear coal bunker, but instead coal was stored on the rear of the left-hand side tank which was given a box-shaped upward extension, although additional coal was usually piled up further forward on the tank top and on the firebox as this picture shows. No. 68129 was one of five in the class and was built at Stratford in January 1921 where it was used in the Locomotive Works until withdrawal in December 1963. Note the 'N7' flowerpot-pattern chimney which it had from June 1949 onwards and the dead, or dumb, buffers fitted. The draincocks on this engine were particularly prone to damage on the inset works track which was usually an inch or two below the stone paving sets. The five-plank wagon, W34907, carries a plaque stating 'Not to be Hump Shunted'.

CHAPTER 11 - STRATFORD SHED, WORKS AND TEMPLE MILLS YARD

Quite independent of the running shed there was a two-road shed used to provide shunting engines for the Works. This usually housed the former GER 'J68/9' tanks and their predecessors that were in departmental service for this function, but occasionally something bigger was found in there – on one occasion it was a 9F! Presumably some Works attention was being carried out. On Sunday January 21st 1962 'J20' 0-6-0 No. 64692 stands outside the Works Shed. Although allocated to Stratford from November 1960 it had been withdrawn in September 1961 but its tender toolbox is open and it looks like it was still being steamed as a temporary works shunter. Adjacent in the small shed (it only held four six-coupled tanks) is Departmental No. 45, formerly 'J69' No. 68543, which worked as a departmental shunter from 1959 until withdrawn in September 1962.

'Y11' Simplex 4-wheel petrol engine No 15098 on 11th October 1956, shortly after withdrawal. It had been purchased by the Great Eastern Railway from the Motor Rail and Tram Company, Simplex Works in Bedford in 1919 and added to L&NER Running Stock in September 1925. It was numbered 8430 in 1930 and No 8188 in 1946 and was therefore allocated BR number 68188 but never carried this and became No 15098 in May 1949. From 1925 almost until withdrawal, it shunted the yard at Brentwood where the name *Peggy* was initially bestowed upon it, allegedly the name of the horse it replaced, although it had been removed by 1933. No. 15098 had a wooden cab with a curved roof and was powered by a 40 bhp Dorman engine. It was used briefly used at Stratford to shunt the Carriage & Wagon Works.

K.L. Cook/Rail Archive Stephenson

English Electric Type '3' No. D6725 in the mid-1960s inside the Engine Repair Shop which had been refurbished in 1958 to deal with diesel maintenance, accommodating up to eighteen locomotives. No. D6725 went new to Stratford from Vulcan Foundry in August 1961 and was there until April 1966 when it moved to March. It remained on the Great Eastern until February 1974 when it was transferred to Thornaby and renumbered to 37025. After withdrawal in 1999, it was purchased for preservation by the 'Scottish Thirty-Seven Group' and has since operated on several heritage lines as well as on the National Network for Colas since 2016.

Temple Mills

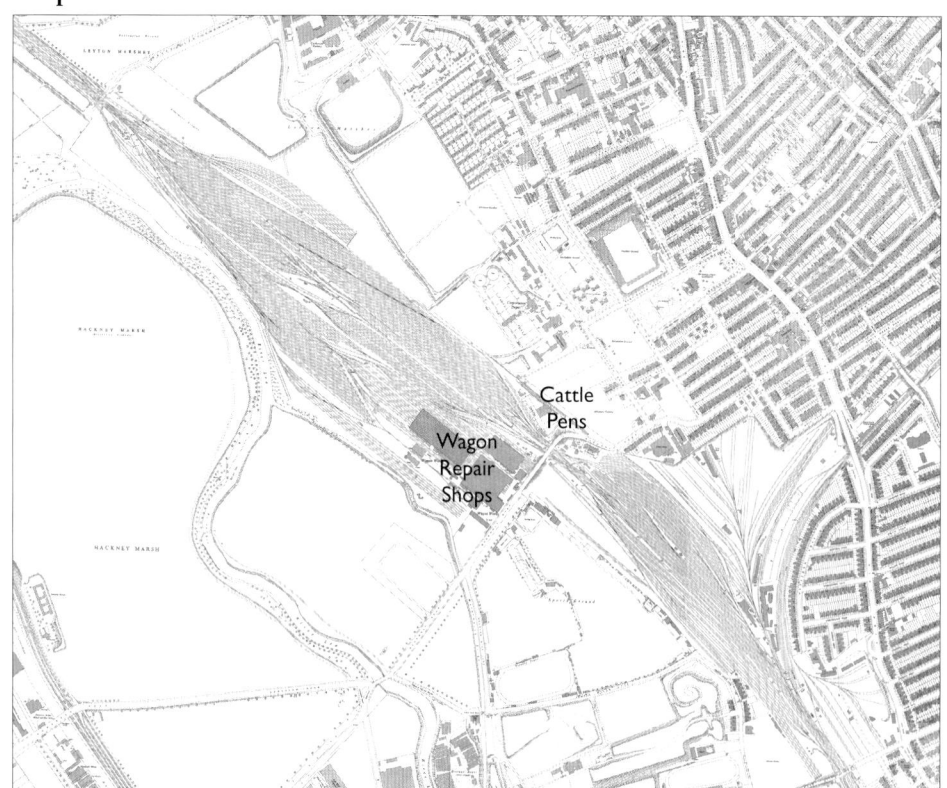

Temple Mills was north of Stratford station on the Lea Valley line, the original route to Cambridge. The yard developed in a piecemeal fashion such that by the early 20th century it comprised eight separate yards which required a considerable amount of short trip working between them. Nothing really changed until 1954 when work began on the construction of a modern hump yard which was completed in September 1958.

The hump closed in 1982 by which date the almost derelict yard was handling only around 200 wagons each day compared with about 4,000 in 1970, and the Wagon Works closed in 1983. Today, most of the area formerly occupied by the Yard was used to create the East Village built as part of the 2012 Olympics development.

Left: The map shows the layout with eight separate yards before the 1950s modernisation.

Viewed from the Ruckholt Road bridge, Midland Railway condenser-fitted '3F' 0-6-0T No. 47208 passes through Temple Mills towards Stratford with a transfer freight from the London Midland Region on 23rd September 1954. It was built by Vulcan Foundry in 1900 and was allocated to Cricklewood until August 1956. Note the new permanent way turnout common crossings and switches loaded into the wagon and cattle in the dock on the right – it was a requirement to regularly feed and water animals when in transit. The main line ran through the middle of the yard until it was rebuilt as a hump marshalling yard in the late 1950s when it was diverted to run adjacent to the Wagon Shops which are off-picture to the left.

CHAPTER 11 - STRATFORD SHED, WORKS AND TEMPLE MILLS YARD

'J39/3' 0-6-0 No. 64985 sets off northbound from Temple Mills yard, also on 23rd September 1954. The signal box is Temple Mills South which was closed in 1958 when the new Temple Mills East box was opened; the yard is very overgrown considering how busy it is. No. 64985 was one of the last four of the class, not entering traffic until July 1941, and was allocated to Stratford between September 1952 and November 1955.

North British Type '1' 800 bhp Bo-Bo No. D8400 in the modernised Temple Mills yard on 12th May 1959. In the background is the Control Tower from where the points and electro-pneumatic secondary retarders were operated, the wagons having been slowed automatically by the primary retarders as they came down from the hump. Over seventy lighting towers were constructed and there were almost fifty sidings to handle the through traffic, divided into eight 'fans'.

Lea Bridge

'J20' 0-6-0 No. 64697 from March shed has left Temple Mills yard with a train of coal empties destined for the East Midlands coalfield and is passing Lea Bridge Gas Works heading towards Lea Bridge station on 14th March 1958. In the background the new signal box is being commissioned and extensive alterations to the track layout are underway. Note the Permanent Way look-out man in the foreground with his enamel 'Look Out' armband.

On the same day, Midland Railway '3F' 0-6-0T No. 47202 is crossing over to the goods lines whilst approaching Temple Mills from the north having passed through Lea Bridge station. The original booking hall, later replaced by a portacabin, is on the overbridge but is obscured by smoke. The large 1950s brick building was a parcels depot with its own siding and was the main generator of revenue for the station; it lasted until the mid-1970s.

12 – Stratford to Ilford

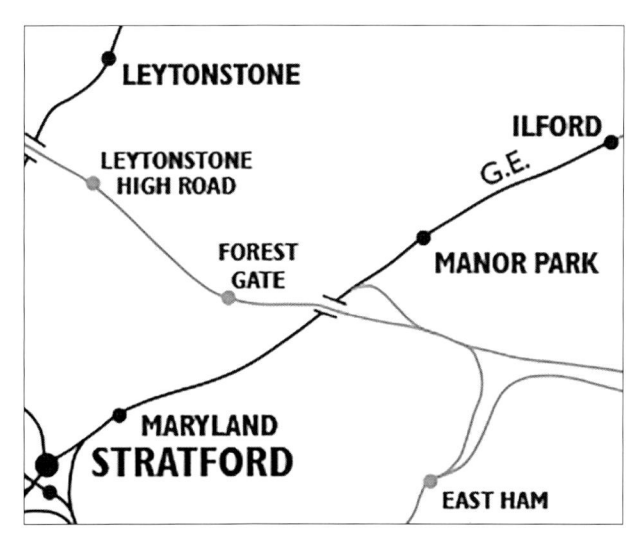

The line from Stratford to Ilford was part of the main line to Colchester and Norwich and was opened by the Eastern Counties Railway between London and Romford in 1839. Its first permanent terminus at Shoreditch was opened in 1840, and this was replaced by Liverpool Street in 1874/5. As traffic grew in the late 19th century and early 20th century, the line between Stratford and Ilford became increasingly congested despite its quadrupling in the mid-1890s. The suburban services to Shenfield via Ilford were not part of the "Jazz" re-organisation in 1920, and although a similar exercise was planned by the GER it was not implemented before the 1923 Grouping. Instead, the L&NER eventually opted in 1935 for electrification of the Shenfield service, but this was delayed by World War Two and was not completed until 1949. A new depot to service the electric multiple units was opened to the east of Ilford station and a flyover built to the west at Aldersbrook to carry the Slow Lines over the Fast lines so that they could resume their original position beyond the station; this allowed the Liverpool Street approaches to be remodelled using the east side platforms for the electric services.

Having passed under Angel Lane Bridge, BTH Type '1' No. D8221 with a short 'K' Class freight is about to enter Stratford station from the Ilford direction in late 1960. It had entered service in March and moved to Ipswich in November, returning to Stratford in May 1968 and working from there until withdrawn in March 1971.

Maryland

Hornsey 'N2/2' 0-6-2T No. 69505 on 11th July 1958 at Maryland, formerly Maryland Point until 1940, as it heads away from Stratford towards Ilford with a through goods train. This was an unusual use of lamps because the three-lamp configuration had not been in general use since 1921. No. 69505 has passed under a forest of trolleybus overhead wires in addition to those above its own track. The trams had been withdrawn from the area in around 1952. The condensing apparatus had been removed from No. 69505 in 1947 but it still has a faded Finsbury Park destination board on the bunker. There had been a building over the tracks but all that remains are a couple of fireplaces. Just visible is the parapet of the Cart & Horses public house on the corner of The Grove with Windmill Lane. It was here that Iron Maiden were to play some of their earliest gigs.

Manor Park

'B1' 4-6-0 No. 61363 rushes through Manor Park station with a Down express on 18th February 1958. The North British 1950 built engine had been transferred from Stratford to Colchester in January 1957 although it would return to 30A in late 1959. On the left, 'AM6' EMU No 039 approaching on the Slow line provides less glamorous passenger accommodation. The station originally had only two platforms on the Local lines until the building of the Ilford flyover in the late 1940s and the swapping of the Main and Local lines.

Ilford

Stratford 'J20' 0-6-0 No. 64682 runs through Ilford station heading towards Stratford in June 1959. It was built in September 1922, rebuilt with a round-topped firebox Diagram 25A boiler into 'J20/1' in August 1947 and withdrawn in September 1960.

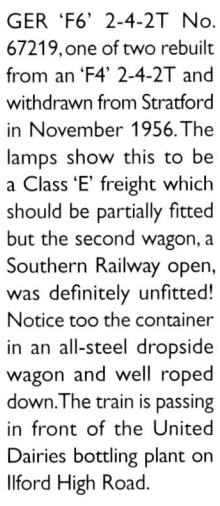

GER 'F6' 2-4-2T No. 67219, one of two rebuilt from an 'F4' 2-4-2T and withdrawn from Stratford in November 1956. The lamps show this to be a Class 'E' freight which should be partially fitted but the second wagon, a Southern Railway open, was definitely unfitted! Notice too the container in an all-steel dropside wagon and well roped down. The train is passing in front of the United Dairies bottling plant on Ilford High Road.

Class '37' No. D6960 with a single four-character display heads the 4F6x Freightliner from Felixstowe heading east towards Stratford passes in front of the Aldersbrook flyover on 22nd August 1969. The flyover was part of the L&NER Shenfield electrification project and was built to transpose the local tracks over the main lines between Ilford and Stratford; the spire peeking out in front of the train is from St. Michael & All Angels Church. No. D6960 was originally allocated to Sheffield Darnall in January 1965, and then Wath later in the year, before moving to Stratford in July 1967. It was renumbered as 37260 in December 1973 and ended its days in Scotland named *Radio Highland* where it was withdrawn in August 1989 after serious fire damage.

In original green livery but with full yellow ends, Class '31' No. D5679 with an Up express on 25th August 1969. It had been transferred to Stratford two months earlier and was there until October 1970 when it went to March for the third time. It was going to be preserved at the Churnet Valley Railway in 2002 but a Class '73' electro-diesel was substituted and as No. 31442 it was cut-up in 2005.

On the same day, but running in the opposite direction, an earlier Class '37', No. 6744, with split headcode panels and newly repainted in British Rail Corporate Blue livery. It had been transferred from Tinsley to March in April 1966 and would then to Stratford in September 1973, before renumbering as No. 37044 in 1974 and 37710 in 1988. It was allocated for Special Projects use in Italy in 2002 but did not go overseas.

Above: Ilford Car Sheds, to the east of the station on the site of Ilford carriage sidings and locomotive shed, which historically had been the base for Shenfield line suburban trains, was opened as part of the Shenfield electrification project. What appears to be just the Driving Trailer of 'AM8' unit No. 143 but is actually the whole unit due to the track curvature, stands outside the cleaning shed in the early 1960s. The three roads could each hold a nine-car Shenfield train as did the inspection shed through which the train first passed.

Driving Trailer Second Only No. E65662 of 'AM6' EMU No. 062 at Ilford in around 1961. The unpowered driving trailers, which did not have a roof-mounted pantograph unlike the Driving Brake Motor Seconds at the other end, were built by Birmingham Railway Carriage & Wagon Co. whereas the other two coaches in the sets came from Metropolitan Cammell. This picture shows the rather stylish original unit numbering on a circular 'Paddle' and the five domino-style route indicator lights. The four white lights at the corners indicated, in nine combinations, the route (or train type if a special, parcels or empty stock); the red light in the centre was the tail light.

13 – Hackney Downs to Brimsdown

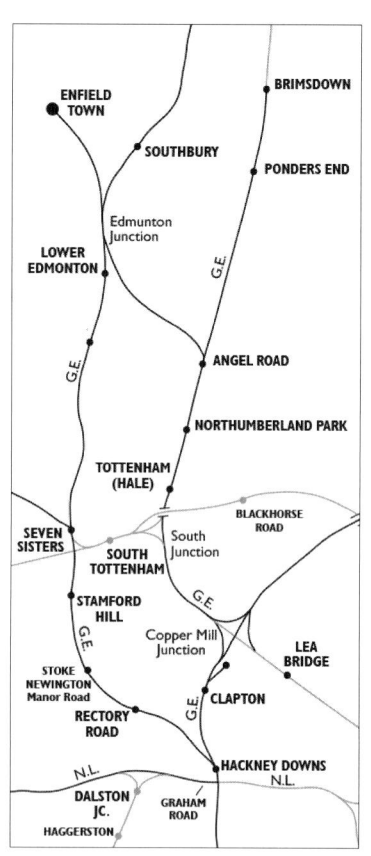

In 1840 the Northern & Eastern Railway opened the Lea Valley line using a track gauge of 5ft from a junction with the Eastern Counties Railway at Stratford to Broxbourne; shortly after it reached Bishop's Stortford and Hertford. It was converted to standard gauge in 1844 and became part of the Eastern Counties Railway which built onwards to Cambridge, opening in 1845.

The line from Bethnal Green Junction to Stoke Newington opened in May 1872 as the first part of a direct line to Enfield Town and the section through Clapton to Copper Mill Junction followed a month later, completing a more direct route to Cambridge which avoided Stratford; Enfield Town was reached in August.

Clapton

'L1' 2-6-4T No. 67733 with the 9.52am Hertford East-Liverpool Street at Clapton on 6th December 1958. It was built by the North British Locomotive Co. in November 1948 and was allocated to Stratford until February 1959. *K.L. Cook/Rail Archive Stephenson*

'B2' 4-6-0 No. 61614 *Castle Hedingham* on the 12.24pm Liverpool Street-Cambridge at Clapton on 24th January 1959. Castle Hedingham is a village in the Colne Valley near Halstead famous for the Norman-built Hedingham Castle. No. 61614 was one of the ten Thompson two-cylinder rebuilds from Gresley's three-cylinder 'B17' class which used the same Diagram 100A boiler as the 'B1' 4-6-0 and were given larger capacity ex-NER 'C7' 4-4-2 4,125 gallon, 5½ ton tenders. *Castle Hedingham* was modified in 1946 and was withdrawn from Cambridge in June 1959. *K.L. Cook/Rail Archive Stephenson*

CHAPTER 13 - HACKNEY DOWNS TO BRIMSDOWN

'B12/3' 4-6-0 No. 61580 with the 9.12am Ely-Liverpool Street at Clapton on 24th January 1959, only a few weeks before withdrawal on 2nd March. It was the last 'B12' built, entering service from Beyer Peacock & Co. in October 1928 as L&NER No. 8580 and fitted with Lentz oscillating cam poppet valve gear. Only four years later it was rebuilt with a larger diameter boiler with round-top firebox and conventional long-travel piston valves. Clapton Goods & Coal Depot on the right had only two sidings but serviced a healthy volume of traffic at this time; it was in use until December 1964.

K.L. Cook/Rail Archive Stephenson

The driver has a good view over the top of the tender of Worsdell 'J15' 0-6-0 No. 65464 with an Up Class 'E' freight at Clapton on 21st March 1959. It had been built by the GER in 1912 and struggled on into its fiftieth year before withdrawal in September 1962. *K.L. Cook/Rail Archive Stephenson*

Copper Mill Junction

'Britannia' 4-6-2 No. 70010 *Owen Glendower* on an Up express at Copper Mill Junction in the early 1950s. It was allocated to Norwich from new in 1951 until December 1961. In 1953 the Cambridge line expresses were re-organised in a similar way to the Ipswich and Norwich services in 1951 when more Pacifics were introduced, although not with such a spectacular impact because of the nature of this route.

WD 'Austerity' 2-8-0 No. 90474 while allocated to March between June 1950 and October 1953, with a southbound Class 'F' unfitted freight on its way to Temple Mills yard passes Copper Mill Junction signal box. The built-up embankment of Warwick Reservoir East is in the right background. No. 90474 was built for the War Department by Vulcan Foundry in 1944 and became L&NER No. 3153 in April 1947 before receiving its BR number in October 1950.

Coming down from South Tottenham Junction '4F' 0-6-0 No. 43964 on a transfer freight for Temple Mills in the early 1950s. The large vertical cylinder in front of the cab is the vacuum reservoir for the Hudd AWS, which was needed for the locomotive to work over the former London Tilbury & Southend lines. No. 43964 was built for the Midland Railway by Armstrong, Whitworth in 1921 and was allocated to Kentish Town from 1946 until 1962. Its Johnson tender is piled high with some very large lumps of coal; this tender was replaced by a LM&SR standard 3,500 gallon tender in September 1957.

Tottenham South Junction

'Britannia' 4-6-2 No. 70003 *John Bunyan* on a Cambridge express at Tottenham South Junction in the mid-1950s.

Northumberland Park

'L1' 2-6-4T No. 67725 with a northbound local at Northumberland Park on 2nd June 1959. It is passing Barnett Foster Ltd Essence Distillers – a manufacturer of bottling machinery and of essences for soft drinks, etc. No. 67725 went to Neasden from new in June 1948 but moved to Stratford in early 1949 and stayed there until withdrawn in December 1960.

Angel Road

Stratford 'J20' 0-6-0 No. 64689 approaches Angel Road with a southbound transfer freight to Temple Mills on 5th September 1959. The class was introduced in 1920 and had many parts in common with the 'B12' 4-6-0 including boiler, cylinders, pistons, rods and valve gear. From 1943 onwards the original Belpaire fireboxes were replaced with a round-topped firebox; No. 64689 was the last to be dealt with, in July 1951.

CHAPTER 13 - HACKNEY DOWNS TO BRIMSDOWN

Three more pictures taken at Angel Road on 5th September 1959. 'L1' 2-6-4T No. 67704 passes Angel Road Junction signal box with a southbound service. It was one of the early members of the class entering service with its planned L&NER number 9003 in January 1948 before being renumbered to 67704 in April 1948. The line curving away to the left was the original Eastern Counties branch to Enfield.

Another 'L1' 2-6-4T No. 67727 departing from Angel Road station with a northbound train. It was opened in 1840 as 'Edmonton', changed to 'Water Lane' in 1849 before becoming Angel Road in 1864. The booking hall above the tracks was accessed from North Circular Road which crosses the line at the far end of the platform.

'N7/3' 0-6-2T No. 69728 approaches Angel Road Junction with a southbound service formed of a single 'Quint-Art' set. It was built in October 1928 as No 2626 with long-travel valve gear and a round-topped firebox and was originally fitted with condensing apparatus for use on the Metropolitan Widened Lines but this was removed in 1937. The line to Edmonton and on to Enfield Town curves away to the left.

Ponders End

Two pictures of an unidentified BTH Type '1' at 1 Ponders End on an engineers' train associated with electrification work in 1968. *Tony Wilkins*

Brimsdown

Early in 1968, No. D8238 shunts 16-ton mineral wagons at Ponders End gas works to make up a trainload of empties for a return working. It went into store in August and was withdrawn at the end of September.
Tony Wilkins

An unidentified North British Locomotive Co. Type '1' shunts a rake of hopper wagons into the exchange sidings for Brimsdown power station in around 1968. *Tony Wilkins*

14 – Hackney Downs to Chingford

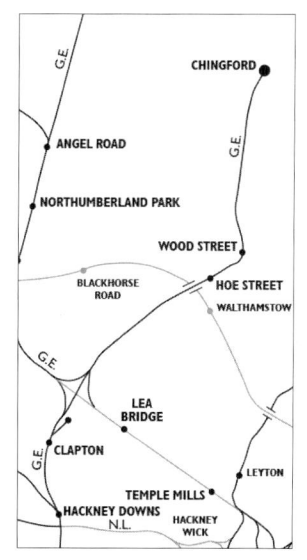

The line from Hackney Downs reached Chingford in 1873 and was soon extended by ¾ mile to the site which the station occupied from 1878, the first station becoming a goods and coal depot. The new station was intended to be a through station continuing to High Beech, three miles to the north, and although the GER had obtained the necessary powers, the company's poor financial position at the time saw these lapse.

Over the first half century of the line, extensive building took place particularly around Walthamstow and Chingford itself changed from a small village to a commuter town. The introduction of the "Jazz" service in 1920 reinforced this, with the population more than doubling between 1921 and 1931. The L&NER made some modest improvements including resignalling with three-aspect electric colour lights and additional carriage sidings at Chingford, but the major change came with electrification under British Railways' 1955 Modernisation Plan. The electric train service came into operation on Monday 14th November 1960 although technical difficulties with the new EMUs saw some steam operation until late 1961.

Clapton

Two 'N7/5' 0-6-2Ts pass at Clapton on 6th December 1958. On the left is No. 69653 with the 12.18pm Chingford-Liverpool Street meeting No. 69646 with the 12.19pm Liverpool Street-Chingford. The Clapton Goods & Coal Depot, as proclaimed in the large blue enamel sign at the entrance, was still quite busy at this date.
K.L. Cook/Rail Archive Stephenson

An Immaculate 'N7/4' 0-6-2T No. 69604 with the 10.20am Liverpool Street-Chingford at Clapton on 21st March 1959. It is hard to believe that it would be withdrawn less than six months after this picture was taken. No. 69604 had five different numbers during its thirty-eight years in service. It was built in September 1921 as GER No. 1004, renumbered by the L&NER in 1924 as 8004 and then as 7982 in August 1944 and as 9604 in December 1946 before its final incarnation as 69604 in March 1948. Originally built without superheating, this was added in 1929 and the Belpaire firebox was replaced by an L&NER standard round-topped firebox in 1941.
K.L. Cook/Rail Archive Stephenson

Hoe Street

Two schoolboys chat with the driver of 'N7/5' 0-6-2T No. 69647 as it waits at Hoe Street with a train from Chingford to Liverpool Street in around 1958. Note the early GPO postman's delivery cart sitting under the canopy. The station was renamed Walthamstow Central in May 1968. Five-car 'Quint-Art' sets were sufficient for off-peak services with ten-car trains only used for rush-hour services. Emblems Furnishing Stores stands on Hoe Street above the footbridge.

Wood Street

An unidentified 'N7' arrives at Wood Street with a southbound train on 13th June 1958. Another 'N7' rests in the engine shed which dated from pre-1920 when most trains from Liverpool Street terminated there. A sub-shed of Stratford with its allocation, which numbered fourteen 'N7' 0-6-2Ts in 1952, therefore carrying 30A shedplates, the shed was demolished immediately after electrification and the site cleared.

CHAPTER 14 - HACKNEY DOWNS TO CHINGFORD

'N7/4' No. 69608 departs from Wood Street with a train to Liverpool Street on 13th June 1958, only two months before it was withdrawn. Note the ground frame controlling the entrance to the coal depot on the right; there was another one covering the entrance to the engine shed.

'N7/4/' 69611 waits at Wood Street with a Down train on 13th June 1958. It was the last of the class built without superheating and retained its short-travel valves; it was rebuilt with a round-topped firebox in 1940 and was withdrawn in November 1960.

'N7/5' 0-6-2T No. 69626 arriving at Wood Street with a ten-coach train to Liverpool Street on 13th June 1958. It was built at Gorton in 1925 and was in service until June 1959. Note on the left a chalked board telling passengers 'No ramp – please use stairs'.

Chingford

'N7/5' 0-6-2T No. 69652 departs for Liverpool Street from Chingford on 19th May 1957. It was the first of twenty of the class built by Robert Stephenson & Co. in 1925/6 and was in traffic until December 1960. The extensive carriage sidings on the left were constructed in 1920 for the introduction of the "Jazz" service. In the mid-1950s Chingford was served by eighty-four trains each day with a journey time for the 10½ miles to Liverpool Street of 26½ minutes for semi-fasts stopping only at four stations and 34½ minutes for those calling at all nine stations.

CHAPTER 14 - HACKNEY DOWNS TO CHINGFORD

'N7/3' 0-6-2T No. 69700 at Chingford on 17th September 1960, two months prior to the official start of the electrified service and three months before it was taken out of traffic.

'N7/3' 0-6-2T No. 69723 at Chingford on 1st October 1960. Although the electric service was introduced on 14th November, technical problems saw steam working continue on some trains into 1961 and No. 69723 itself remained in service until September of that year.

15 – Hackney Downs to Enfield Town

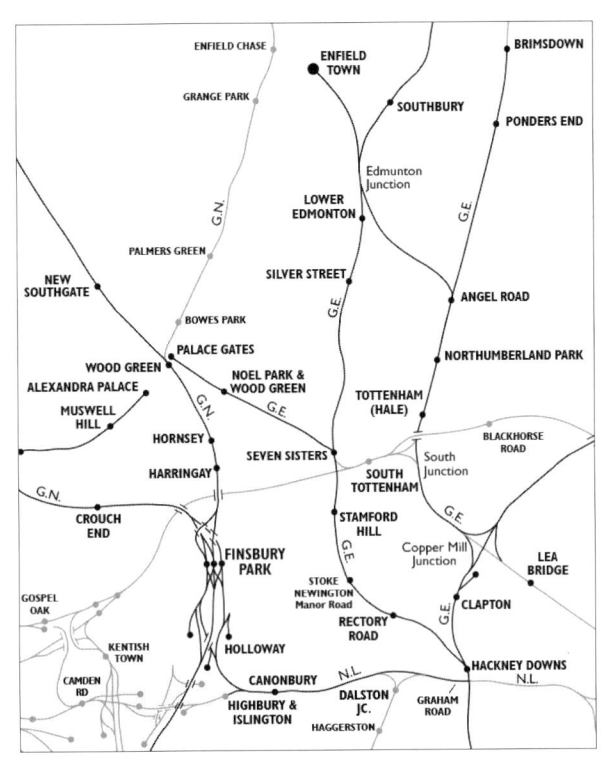

The Eastern Counties Railway, which became part of the Great Eastern Railway in 1862, opened a branch to Enfield from its Lea Valley line at Angel Road in 1849. However, it would be over two decades before Enfield Town was linked on a more direct route to London than via Stratford. This had to wait until the line from Bethnal Green Junction via Hackney Downs to Edmonton was opened to passenger traffic in 1872.

In the years up to the end of the 19th century people moved from inner-London out to the new suburbs and the service to Enfield Town increased significantly but it began to decline after the turn of the century because of competition from electric tramcars. The introduction of the "Jazz" in July 1920 revolutionised the service to Enfield Town and further improvements followed in the 1920s with the 'N7' 0-6-2Ts and 'Quint-Art' rolling stock.

The opening of the Piccadilly Line extension to nearby Cockfosters reduced traffic in the 1930s and there were only minor infrastructure and signalling improvements on the route until the end of the 1950s. However, this was to change in 1960 when an electrified service on the Enfield, Chingford, Hertford East and Bishop's Stortford lines came into operation on Monday 14th November. Technical problems with the electrical equipment of the new 'AM5' units delayed the full implementation until June 1962 when a ten-minute frequency off-peak service was introduced. However, the investment did not result in higher passenger numbers and the service was reduced in 1965 and was impacted further by the opening of the Victoria Line tube to Walthamstow in 1968.

Derby 'Lightweight' two-car DMU, with Driving Trailer Composite No E79621 leading, at Rectory Road on 20th July 1957. The station was opened in 1872 and changed very little over the following century until it was completely rebuilt in the 1980s.

Stoke Newington - Manor Road

Manor Road sidings were immediately north of Stoke Newington station and had a small, two-road goods and coal yard accessed from a loop on the Down line. 'N7/5' 0-6-2T No. 69658 has just left Stoke Newington with a Down Enfield "Jazz" on 11th November 1958.
K.L. Cook/Rail Archive Stephenson

'N7/3' 0-6-2T No. 69683 passes Manor Road sidings with an Enfield Town to Liverpool Street train on 4th April 1959. This was the second of the engines built by W. Beardmore & Co. with long-travel valve gear and left-hand drive; originally it was only steam braked but Westinghouse equipment was added in 1940, and a round-topped firebox in December 1954.
K.L. Cook/Rail Archive Stephenson

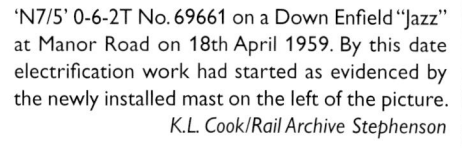

'N7/5' 0-6-2T No. 69661 on a Down Enfield "Jazz" at Manor Road on 18th April 1959. By this date electrification work had started as evidenced by the newly installed mast on the left of the picture.
K.L. Cook/Rail Archive Stephenson

'N7/3' 0-6-2T No. 69702 on a Down Enfield "Jazz" at Manor Road on 4th April 1959. A solitary 5-plank fitted merchandise wagon which has probably brought in engineering materials stands in the coal yard which remained in use until the end of 1964.
K.L. Cook/Rail Archive Stephenson

'L1' 2-6-4T No. 67729 on a Down Enfield "Jazz" at Manor Road on 4th April 1959. The 2-6-4Ts were not often used on the Enfield or Chingford services because their high bunkers were hard to coal without the benefit of a hopper.
K.L. Cook/Rail Archive Stephenson

CHAPTER 15 - HACKNEY DOWNS TO ENFIELD TOWN

'N7/3' 0-6-2T No. 69681 on a Down Enfield "Jazz" at Manor Road on 18th April 1959. It was the last of the class built at Gorton works, entering service in February 1928 and was rebuilt with a round-topped firebox in April 1952. The coal yard is busier than in the previous pictures but it is interesting that there is only one steel mineral wagon in use – perhaps the local coal merchants requested wooden wagons?

K.L. Cook/Rail Archive Stephenson

Seven Sisters

'N7/5' 0-6-2T No. 69670 at Seven Sisters on a Liverpool Street train in the late 1950s before electrification work had started. It was built by R. Stephenson & Co. in January 1926 and was fitted with a round-top firebox when it became an 'N7/5' in November 1950. Seven Sisters was 5 miles 50 chains from Liverpool Street and was opened in July 1872 for the Enfield line and was extended from two to four platforms for the Palace Gates branch in 1874.

A decorated 'N7/5' 0-6-2T, No. 69658, with the 12.52pm Liverpool Street-Enfield Town approaches Seven Sisters station on 11th October 1958. The track joining on the left curved up a sharp incline round from South Tottenham station on the former Tottenham & Hampstead Junction which passed below the GER line. The advertisements on the right of the train are interesting, ranging from Pepsi-Cola to 'Electric cooking – quick-automatic-up to date' and the first appearance at the Regal Edmonton of the modestly billed 'America's Greatest Vocalists', The Hi-Los, a four-piece vocal harmony group. There is an Austin garage fronting onto Seven Sisters Road in the centre of the picture.   *K.L. Cook/Rail Archive Stephenson*

Even though it was a Sunday, it was washing day for the ladies in Westerfield Road as another well-cared for 'N7/5' 0-6-2T No. 69663 leaves Seven Sisters with the 1.16pm Enfield Town-Liverpool Street on 11th October 1958. The main station buildings and entrance were on the Enfield line linked by a subway to the Palace Gates platforms on the left which were only provided with small shelters.   *K.L. Cook/Rail Archive Stephenson*

Lower Edmonton

Class '305' EMU No. 433 at Lower Edmonton in the early 1970s. This was one of the fifty-two three-car units built at York for the Enfield and Chingford electrification in 1960. The station was opened as Edmonton in July 1872, was renamed Lower Edmonton in July 1883 and became Edmonton Green in 1992.

Enfield Town

'N7/5' 0-6-2T No. 69670 arrives at Enfield Town from Liverpool Street while another 'N7/5' No. 69663 waits to move out from the carriage sidings. Both engines were among the twenty built for the L&NER by R. Stephenson & Co. with the latter being taken out of service upon electrification in November 1960 while the former lasted until September 1961.

Two 'N7' 0-6-2Ts, Nos 69693 and 69665, wait for their next turn of duty in the engine yard at Enfield on 12th August 1959. The large board on the right informs passengers of the forthcoming modernisation: 'ELECTRIFICATION OF LINE – PROGRESS BY GREAT EASTERN'. The rebuilding of Enfield Town station was one of only two structural improvements undertaken on the line, along with a new power-operated signal box installed at Hackney Downs. The houses to the right are at the end of Chalkwell Park Avenue and Lyndhurst Avenue – how often did the washing go in slightly smutty if crews were not paying attention. Notice how the signal wires running vertically alongside the bunker on the right drop to horizontal alongside the stabling point.

CHAPTER 15 - HACKNEY DOWNS TO ENFIELD TOWN

With two of the new 'AM5' electric units ready to take over the "Jazz" service in November, 'N7/5' 0-6-2T No. 69642 waits for departure time at Enfield Town on 17th September 1960. The station had been rebuilt in 1958 as part of the electrification project with a 418ft long concrete and glass awning on the island platform.

Now classified under TOPS as a '305', EMU No. 423 forms the front half of a six-car set at Enfield Town on a Liverpool Street service in November 1969. On the right are the EMU stabling sidings which were built on the site of the former goods yard.

16 – Stratford to Palace Gates

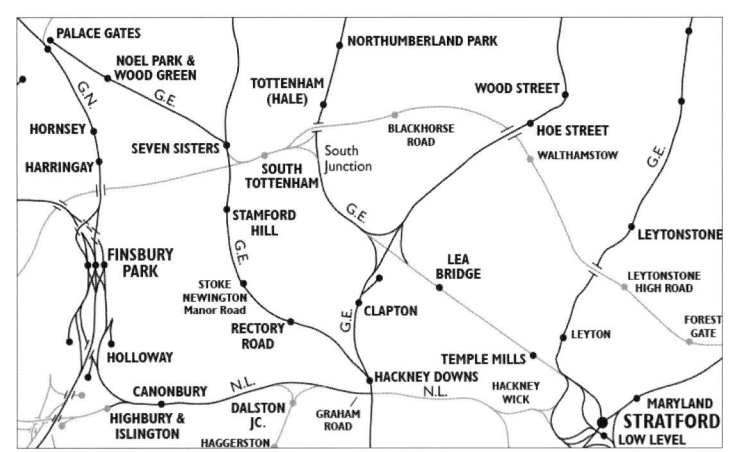

Palace Gates was a GER outpost in the middle of GNR territory intended to provide a rival service for what was envisaged as lucrative business to Alexandra Palace. The two miles sixteen chains long branch from Seven Sisters opened in October 1878.

In July 1920 as part of the "Jazz" re-organisation, the GER introduced a half-hourly off-peak shuttle service between Seven Sisters and Palace Gates which connected with the Enfield trains at Seven Sisters. During rush hour, Palace Gates had three through trains from Liverpool Street but these ended in 1939 and were not restored after the War; the shuttle service was reintroduced in mid-1948 but was discontinued in September 1951.

The other services on the branch were from Stratford and North Woolwich which began in 1887 and lasted until 1963. The 12½ mile journey took around forty-two minutes, calling at all stations, and by the late 1930s there were fourteen trains each day on weekdays. Around half a dozen trains each way ran during the peak-hour until the service was cut-back to Tottenham Hale in January 1963. It became the final outpost of steam working on the former Great Eastern lines in the London area.

Left: Worsdell 'G5' 0-4-4T No. 67269 at Seven Sisters after arrival with the Palace Gates shuttle service in 1950. It was built by the North Eastern Railway in March 1896 and was one of three of the class transferred from the North East to Stratford for use on the Seven Sisters-Palace Gates and the Epping-Ongar services, replacing the 'F7' 2-4-2Ts on the Palace Gates shuttle. No. 67269 arrived in May 1944 and was fitted with push-pull gear in February 1945. All three 0-4-4Ts were transferred to Cambridge in July 1951 to work the Audley End-Bartlow service and the Palace Gates push-pulls were discontinued. The three-coach train behind No. 67269 is made up of former GER main line bogie clerestories which had arrived on the branch in 1926.

'N7/3' 0-6-2T No. 69686 at Seven Sisters with the 12.28pm Palace Gates-North Woolwich meets a train going to Palace Gates on 11th October 1958. It had been built as L&NER No 2646 in July 1927 by W. Beardmore & Co. and was originally allocated to the former GNR lines at King's Cross until 1939, when it was transferred to Stratford and converted to dual braking to operate on the Westinghouse system used on the Great Eastern. Note the large 401B set number on the rear of the 'Quint-Art' set. The Enfield Town line is on the right. Before the station was resignalled in 1934/5 a 'Syx' auto-stop system had been installed on the Palace Gates Up platform line to prevent trains over-running onto the Enfield tracks since there were no trap points.

K.L. Cook/Rail Archive Stephenson

CHAPTER 16 - STRATFORD TO PALACE GATES

'N7/3' 0-6-2T No. 69686 pulls out of Seven Sisters with the 12.28pm Palace Gates-North Woolwich on 11th October 1958. No. 69686 was at Stratford until withdrawn in September 1961, except for two short spells away at Colchester and Parkeston Quay in 1959 and 1960. In the final year of the service Brush Type '2' diesels took over until closure to passengers in January 1963. *K.L. Cook/Rail Archive Stephenson*

Noel Park and Wood Green

North Eastern Railway Worsdell 'G5' 0-4-4T No. 67269 waits at Noel Park and Wood Green on its way to Seven Sisters in 1950. It was one of three of the class transferred from the North East to work push-pull services on the former Great Eastern lines and allocated to Stratford from May 1948 until July 1951 when it was transferred to Cambridge. Noel Park and Wood Green, originally Green Lanes, was the first, temporary terminus of the branch; its platforms and shelters had been renewed in 1939.

Palace Gates (Wood Green)

'N7/4' 0-6-2T No. 69613 waits to depart from Palace Gates (Wood Green) in the mid-1950s. This was the second of the L&NER built engines, entering service in December 1923, and was at Stratford between November 1953 and October 1957. Its condensing gear was removed in July 1936 and it was rebuilt with a round-topped firebox in December 1941.

A brand new Wickham two-car DMU with a pairing of Motor Brake Second No. E50418 and Driving Trailer Composite No E56173 wait for departure from Palace Gates in 1958. This unit was photographed at Stratford on the same day (see page 141). Palace Gates was built as a through station, and was within stone's throw of the Great Northern main line Wood Green station; it was eventually physically connected to the GNR Hertford Loop in 1930. Freight services on the branch outlasted the passenger service by almost two years.

17 – Stratford to North Woolwich

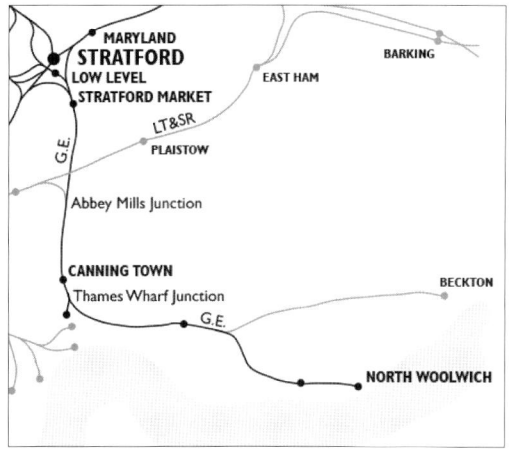

The line from Stratford to North Woolwich was opened in 1847 by the Great Eastern Railway's forerunner, the Eastern Counties Railway, with trains to Liverpool Street or Fenchurch Street; the first service to Palace Gates began in 1887. The line suffered from road competition but was still carrying over ninety weekday trains to and from North Woolwich up to the outbreak of war in 1939, during which it suffered extensive damage, although a shuttle service to Stratford was maintained.

By 1960 there was an hourly service with a ten-minute frequency in the peak periods and in 1962 there were thirty-seven Down trains, six of which started at Palace Gates, one from Cheshunt and the remainder from Stratford Low Level. In the other direction of the thirty-eight trains, nine went through to Palace Gates and the others terminated at Stratford. The 'N7' 0-6-2Ts and 'L1' 2-6-4Ts which had replaced the 'F5's in the late 1950s worked the service until January 1962 when three-car DMUs took over most trains, although some trains continued to be 'N7' worked until September 1962 when they were replaced for a few months by Brush Type '2' diesels.

Stratford Low Level

Holden 'F5' 2-4-2T No. 67203 departing from Stratford Low Level on a North Woolwich train after it had received its BR number and lettering in April 1948 but before its condensing gear was taken off in July 1949. It was built at Stratford Works in 1905 as GER No. 7094 and was withdrawn in 1957. The large building behind the engine is the District Engineer's Offices which were built in 1938 and the curve to the right is to the GER main line; this was never regularly used by passenger trains and was closed in March 1973.

Stratford 'N7/3' 0-6-2T No. 69723 on a North Woolwich service in the late 1950s in the same place as the 'F5'. In addition to a more powerful and modern engine, there is now BR-built stock at the front of the train.

In the first of three pictures taken at Stratford Low Level on 4th February 1961, 'J17' 0-6-0 No. 65567 from Norwich Thorpe with steam leaking badly wheezes through with a freight for the docks. Stratford had a habit of borrowing engines from other sheds for its own use and at this date it seems unlikely that Norwich would miss an old 0-6-0! No. 65567 was built in 1905 as GER No. 1217 and rebuilt to a superheated 'J17' in September 1923 and would work for another eighteen months until withdrawn in August 1962, and was one of a handful of 'J17's to run with a small 2,640 gallon tender until withdrawal. No. 65567 was preserved as part of the National Collection and cosmetically restored to L&NER livery as No. 8217.

'J69/1' 0-6-0T No. 68552 runs briskly through the station with a Class '9' freight. It was withdrawn from Stratford in September 1961 after completing almost seventy years in service. Goods traffic was heavy during the 1950s with a daily total of about sixty trains joining or leaving the branch at Stratford.

Contrasting with the previous picture, BTH Type '1' diesel-electric No. D8234 passes through the Low Level station on 4th February 1961, also working a Class '9' freight. No. D8234 was only in service for less than eleven years and was withdrawn in March 1971.

Stratford Market

'N7/3' 0-6-2T No. 69714 with a train to Stratford in the final few days of Stratford Market station which closed in May 1957. The station canopies had been damaged during the Second World War and were never replaced. The station was opened in 1847 as Stratford Bridge and became Stratford Market in 1880. No. 69714 was built at Doncaster in January 1928 as L&NER No. 2612 and was withdrawn from Stratford in September 1961.

Stratford 'J19/2' 0-6-0 No. 64664 has just passed through Stratford Market station and is heading towards Canning Town on 22nd May 1957. It was built in 1918 as GER No. 1264 and rebuilt in February 1939 with a larger Diagram 28A boiler and round-topped firebox; it was withdrawn from 30A in September 1962. There is a double slip in the foreground interlocked with a ground signal and note the minimal level crossing gates leading into Stratford Market sidings. The large building to the left of the line is the Stratford Fruit and Vegetable depot which had a new lease of life following the fire in December 1964 which destroyed the Bishopsgate depot, handling all the perishables traffic from Europe which arrived at Harwich.

CHAPTER 17 - STRATFORD TO NORTH WOOLWICH

The schoolboy watches Gresley 'J39' 0-6-0 No. 64776 with coal empties heading towards Canning Town south of Stratford Market on 7th June 1956. Strangely, it is displaying express passenger lamp codes, but this may have been a local routing code. No. 64776 was built at Darlington in April 1929 and had been allocated to Stratford since 1946 but would move to Parkeston later in the year. The glass works behind the engine had a wagon tippler used for unloading the large quantities of coal used in the glass-making process.

Canning Town

'N7/5' 0-6-2T No. 69668 with a North Woolwich-Palace Gates train passing under the LT&SR line north of Canning Town on 16th May 1961. It was built by R. Stephenson & Co. in December 1925 and was rebuilt with a round-topped firebox in October 1950. A Morris Minor convertible is parked outside the railway boundary fence on Manor Road.

D.M.C. Hepburne-Scott/Rail Archive Stephenson

Abbey Mills Junction

'B1' 4-6-0 No. 61048 passes Abbey Mills Junction with a freight for Temple Mills on 25th November 1961. This was one of the first batch of the class built for the L&NER by the North British Locomotive Co. and entered service in June 1946. It was allocated to Cambridge at the time of this photograph but was withdrawn from Stratford in June 1962.

K.L. Cook/Rail Archive Stephenson

With Abbey Mills Junction in the distance and the cranes of the George Cohen 600 Group Bidder Street dismantling yard on the right, an unidentified 'L1' 2-6-4T heads a train to Stratford/Palace Gates on 25th November 1961. It is displaying what were normally Class 'H' through freight headlamp codes but local routing codes were used in this area.

K.L. Cook/Rail Archive Stephenson

Thames Wharf Junction

'J19/2' 0-6-0 No. 64667 passes Thames Wharf Junction with an Up freight devoid of any headlamp codes on 28th August 1961. The Stratford allocated engine was within three weeks of withdrawal after forty-two years' service. The signal box had been extended in 1939 and was closed in December 1973.
K.L. Cook/Rail Archive Stephenson

'J20' 0-6-0 No. 64692 with a freight for Stratford at Thames Wharf Junction on 28th August 1961, also within three weeks of withdrawal. Twenty of the class were built between 1920 and 1922 as a more powerful goods engine using the boiler, cylinders and valve gear interchangeable with the 'B12' 4-6-0s which resulted in a long 18ft 10in. wheelbase compared to the 17ft 8in. of their 'J19' predecessors. From 1943 onwards they were all rebuilt with round-topped fireboxes. No. 64692 has passed under the Silvertown Way viaduct and is heading towards Canning Town.
K.L. Cook/Rail Archive Stephenson

'N7/3' 0-6-2T No. 69724 with a Stratford Low Level-North Woolwich train approaching Thames Wharf Junction on 28th August 1961. The bracket signal that it has just passed has an interesting collection of arms. As with the engines in the previous two photographs, it would be withdrawn in mid-September. Above the second carriage stands The Chandelier, a Watney's pub, in Victoria Dock Road. Originally the Victoria Dock Tavern it closed in the early 1990s and has been demolished.
K.L. Cook/Rail Archive Stephenson

North Woolwich

An unidentified 'N7' departs from North Woolwich on a damp and misty 14th January 1956. Note the unusual track layout allowing incoming engines to run around their trains without the stock having to be moved; in earlier times the two tracks in the foreground led onto a turntable. This was destroyed in September 1940 when the station suffered a direct hit from German bombs which also badly damaged the platform canopies; these were cut back almost to the station building.

CHAPTER 17 - STRATFORD TO NORTH WOOLWICH

'N7/3' 0-6-2T No. 69718 stands by North Woolwich signal box on 9th May 1960. The layout of tracks at the station throat allowed incoming trains to use any of the platforms. The shortened platform canopies were completely removed in 1956/57. Note the diesel shunter working in what was still a busy goods yard although it would be rationalised by within five years and was closed together with the signal box in December 1970. No. 69718 was withdrawn from Stratford in December 1960. The station opened on 14th June 1847 as the southern terminus of the Eastern Counties and Thames Junction Railway from Stratford. The Italianate station building was designed by Sir William Tite and is now Grade II listed. After closure the site served as the North Woolwich Old Station Museum until it too closed in 2008. After suffering many years of decay it was acquired in 2021 by the New Covenant Church in Woolwich which plans to renovate and convert the building into a church.

The carriage doors are still open as 'N7/3' 0-6-2T No. 69715 waits for departure time at North Woolwich in June 1960. It also succumbed at the end of 1960. Notice the method of supplying power to the platform lamps.

'L1' 2-6-4T No. 67716 with the 12.10pm North Woolwich-Palace Gates leaves North Woolwich on 25th November 1961. It briefly carried the number 69015 when built in April 1948, the last of the class to have a 69000 number. No. 67716 moved from its original shed, Stratford, to Ipswich in May 1950, returning to the London shed in January 1959 where it stayed until withdrawal in September 1962 when steam working at Stratford ended. The rows of post-war prefabricated bungalows contrast with their high-rise replacements in the background.   *K.L. Cook/Rail Archive Stephenson*

18 – Stratford to Epping and Ongar

The Eastern Counties Railway opened a double track line from Stratford to Loughton in 1856 and the GER extended it as a single track to Epping and Ongar in 1865; the part from Loughton to Epping was doubled in 1893. Commuter traffic developed rapidly from Loughton which had become a middle-class suburb with the highest proportion of first class ticket-holders on the GER. Around fifty trains each way ran on weekdays by the early 1900s; the traffic north of Loughton was much lighter and only a portion of each train went on to Epping and Ongar.

In the early 1930s as part of the 1935-40 London Railways New Works Programme, the Central Line tube was to be extended to Leyton and would then take over the line to Ongar. Work was delayed by the Second World War but tube trains finally reached Leytonstone in May 1947. On 1st January 1948 the London Transport Executive took over responsibility for the whole line to Ongar although steam trains continued to work a shuttle service northward, reducing in extent as electrification advanced until Epping was reached in September 1949. For the next eight years London Transport hired from British Railways a steam shuttle to work between Epping and Ongar until it was decided to extend the electrification to Ongar.

The traffic from Ongar failed to justify the investment, partly because while Epping's population increased threefold in the first six decades of the 20th century, Ongar's fell by 25% and even after the building of new housing several initiatives failed to make the service economic and trains from Epping to Ongar were withdrawn in September 1994 and the line was closed.

The stations at North Weald and Ongar have been taken over and restored by the Epping Ongar Railway with trains running between the two; the heritage line continues to within 100 yards of Epping station and the aim is to eventually run trains through to Epping.

Leytonstone

'N7/1' 0-6-2 No. 9630 at Leytonstone with an Epping shuttle on 5th May 1947, the first day of the electric service. It was built at Gorton as No. 473 in November 1925 and kept its Belpaire firebox until July 1950 when it also received its BR number.
A.W. Croughton/Rail Archive Stephenson

A Central Line tube train for Wood Lane arrives at Leytonstone as 'N7/4' 0-6-2T No. 9616 waits in the adjacent bay platform used for the temporary steam shuttle to Epping in late 1947 or early 1948. It was one of the L&NER built engines, No. 7994, rebuilt with a round-topped firebox in 1942 and was not given its BR number until September 1949. In the right background is the Kirkdale Works, situate in Kirkdale Road, of the London Battery and Cable Co. who were accumulator manufacturers.

Loughton

As part of the electrification project a new station about 250 yards north of the existing station was opened at Loughton in April 1940. It had two island platforms and futuristic concrete architecture using a barrel vault theme for the main building and kidney-shaped flat-slab platform canopy supports; it was given Grade II listing in 1994. London Transport trains did not run through to Loughton until November 1948. 'N7/1' 0-6-2T No. 9634, waiting with an Ongar train alongside a Central Line tube train, was built as No. 828 at Gorton in February 1926, received its BR number in May 1948 and kept its Belpaire firebox until February 1951; although re-numbered on the tank side it had not yet been fitted with a smokebox number plate. *C.R.L. Coles/Rail Archive Stephenson*

Epping

'F5' 2-4-2T No. 67202 with the Ongar-Epping push-and-pull approaching Epping on 8th May 1955. It had been fitted with a steam brake and vacuum-operated push-and-pull gear in 1949 and was withdrawn from Stratford in December 1957 following the electrification of the Epping to Ongar line. *J.F. Davies/Rail Archive Stephenson*

GER 'F5' 2-4-2T No. 67213 at Epping in the mid-1950s behind a Central Line train from West Ruislip which terminated there. No. 67213 was built in 1907 and had been fitted with a steam brake and vacuum-operated push-and-pull gear in 1949; No. 67213 was withdrawn at the end of 1955. Although both lines in the station were electrified, only the Down line was used by London Transport trains except for one early morning train which was used to test the current on the Up line.

GER 'F5' 2-4-2T No. 67213 at Epping with an Ongar train in April 1954. The line to Ongar became single from beyond the road bridge in the background of this picture and was not electrified until 1957. Platform canopies were never provided for the station although the footbridge originally had a roof.

GER 'F5' 2-4-2T No. 67213 tops up its tanks at Epping in April 1954. The engines used on the push-pull were all allocated to Stratford. The water crane was installed by British Railways on the Up platform when the London Transport trains took over the Down platform.

Below: Epping Shed with 'J15' 0-6-0 No. 5455 alongside two 'F5' 2-4-2Ts Nos 67200 and 67193 in 1950. The two-road sub-shed of Stratford, rebuilt in a 'blockhouse' style during 1949, was used by the engines on the Ongar push-pull but also had a 50ft turntable which could accommodate the 'J15' 0-6-0 used for the daily goods train on the line; it closed in 1957 when the electrification was extended to Ongar.
E.V. Fry/Rail Archive Stephenson

North Weald

GER 'F5' 2-4-2T No. 67200 with the 10.51am Ongar-Epping passes classmate No. 67218 on the 10.56am from Epping at North Weald on 20th April 1957. Both engines became surplus after the electrification of the line from Epping was completed in November 1957. As part of the modernisation work at North Weald a passing loop was built in 1949 replacing an existing siding and a second platform constructed, allowing peak-hour trains to run at twenty minute intervals.
K.L.Cook/Rail Archive Stephenson

Blake Hall

Above: 'F5' 2-4-2T No. 67193 at Blake Hall on 1st April 1956. After electrification in 1957, this remote station was apparently the least used of all London Transport's stations and was closed in October 1981, by then averaging less than twenty passengers a day. No. 67193 itself was withdrawn in November 1957.

'F5' 2-4-2T No. 67203 with the 1.20pm Epping-Ongar leaving Blake Hall on 21st April 1957. The 2-4-2Ts were built by the Great Eastern Railway for its London suburban services and after they were superseded by the 'N7' 0-6-2Ts in the 1920s many found their way onto lighter branch line duties.

K.L. Cook/Rail Archive Stephenson

Ongar

'F5' 2-4-2T No. 67200 waits to leave Ongar with the 12.27pm push-pull train to Epping on 14th April 1957. The coal wagon could be used to top up locomotive supplies. The conductor rails for the forthcoming electrification have been deposited in the four foot before final positioning on their insulators. *K.L. Cook/ Rail Archive Stephenson*

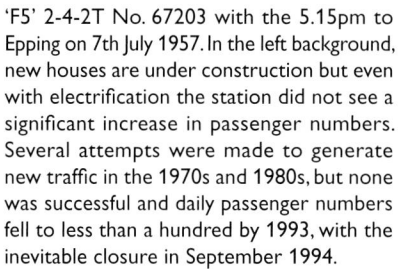

'F5' 2-4-2T No. 67203 with the 5.15pm to Epping on 7th July 1957. In the left background, new houses are under construction but even with electrification the station did not see a significant increase in passenger numbers. Several attempts were made to generate new traffic in the 1970s and 1980s, but none was successful and daily passenger numbers fell to less than a hundred by 1993, with the inevitable closure in September 1994.

The 'F5' 2-4-2Ts, here No. 67202, and the Push-Pull sets were serviced at off-peak times in the yard. There was an inspection pit and fires could be refreshed here, and it was customary to leave the coaches attached for this procedure. Note the old GER coach body on brick plinths used as a store and messroom.
T.G. Hepburn/Rail Archive Stephenson

'F5' 2-4-2T No. 67202 waits to leave Ongar for Epping in 1955. Note the goods shed behind the wall and the spare coaching stock stored in the goods yard. Freight traffic continued after electrification, ceasing in April 1966.
T.G. Hepburn/Rail Archive Stephenson